STIMULANTS

Other Books in the Drug Education Library series:

STIMULANTS

by Pam Walker and Elaine Wood

LUCENT
BOOKS®

THOMSON
™
GALE

San Diego • Detroit • New York • San Francisco • Cleveland
New Haven, Conn. • Waterville, Maine • London • Munich

Cover: Freshly harvested coffee beans from Hawaii.

© 2004 by Lucent Books. Lucent Books is an imprint of The Gale Group, Inc., a division of Thomson Learning, Inc.

Lucent Books® and Thomson Learning™ are trademarks used herein under license.

For more information, contact
Lucent Books
27500 Drake Rd.
Farmington Hills, MI 48331-3535
Or you can visit our Internet site at http://www.gale.com

LIBRARY OF CONGRESS CATALOGING-IN-PUBLICATION DATA

Walker, Pam, 1958–
    Stimulants / by Pam Walker and Elaine Wood.
    v. cm. — (Drug education library)
    Includes bibliographical references and index.
    Contents: A brief history of stimulants—Stimulant—Dangers of stimulant abuse —Treatment for stimulant abuse and addiction—Stimulant trafficking.
    ISBN 1-59018-044-5 (alk. paper)
    1. Stimulants—Juvenile literature. 2. Drug abuse—Juvenile literature. [1. Stimulants. 2. Drug abuse.] I. Wood, Elaine, 1950– . II. Title. III. Series.
    HV5822.A5W35 2004
    362.29'9—dc22

                                                                    2003016735

Printed in the United States of America

Contents

Foreword

The development of drugs and drug use in America is a cultural paradox. On the one hand, strong, potentially dangerous drugs provide people with relief from numerous physical and psychological ailments. Sedatives like Valium counter the effects of anxiety; steroids treat severe burns, anemia, and some forms of cancer; morphine provides quick pain relief. On the other hand, many drugs (sedatives, steroids, and morphine among them) are consistently misused or abused. Millions of Americans struggle each year with drug addictions that overpower their ability to think and act rationally. Researchers often link drug abuse to criminal activity, traffic accidents, domestic violence, and suicide.

These harmful effects seem obvious today. Newspaper articles, medical papers, and scientific studies have highlighted the myriad problems drugs and drug use can cause. Yet, there was a time when many of the drugs now known to be harmful were actually believed to be beneficial. Cocaine, for example, was once hailed as a great cure, used to treat everything from nausea and weakness to colds and asthma. Developed in Europe during the 1880s, cocaine spread quickly to the United States where manufacturers made it the primary ingredient in such everyday substances as cough medicines, lozenges, and tonics. Likewise, heroin, an opium derivative, became a popular painkiller during the late nineteenth century. Doctors and patients flocked to American drugstores to buy heroin, described as the optimal cure for even the worst coughs and chest pains.

As more people began using these drugs, though, doctors, legislators, and the public at large began to realize that they were more damaging than beneficial. After years of using heroin as a painkiller, for example, patients began asking their doctors for larger and stronger doses. Cocaine users reported dangerous side effects, including hallucinations and wild mood shifts. As a result, the U.S. government initiated more stringent regulation of many powerful and addictive drugs, and in some cases outlawed them entirely.

A drug's legal status is not always indicative of how dangerous it is, however. Some drugs known to have harmful effects can be purchased legally in the United States and elsewhere. Nicotine, a key ingredient in cigarettes, is known to be highly addictive. In an effort to meet their bodies' demands for nicotine, smokers expose themselves to lung cancer, emphysema, and other life-threatening conditions. Despite these risks, nicotine is legal almost everywhere.

Other drugs that cannot be purchased or sold legally are the subject of much debate regarding their effects on physical and mental health. Marijuana, sometimes described as a gateway drug that leads users to other drugs, cannot legally be used, grown, or sold in this country. However, some research suggests that marijuana is neither addictive nor a gateway drug and that it might actually benefit cancer and AIDS patients by reducing pain and encouraging failing appetites. Despite these findings and occasional legislative attempts to change the drug's status, marijuana remains illegal.

The Drug Education Library examines the paradox of drugs and drug use in America by focusing on some of the most commonly used and abused drugs or categories of drugs available today. By discussing objectively the many types of drugs, their intended purposes, their effects (both planned and unplanned), and the controversies surrounding them, the books in this series provide readers with an understanding of the complex role drugs and drug use play in American society. Informative sidebars, annotated bibliographies, and organizations to contact lists highlight the text and provide young readers with many opportunities for further discussion and research.

 **Introduction**

Stimulants: At Home and Around the World

A cup of coffee and a hit of cocaine—they seem as different as day and night. Yet coffee (which contains caffeine) and cocaine are chemical relatives, two members of a group of drugs called stimulants. Stimulants are a diverse collection of chemicals that share one important characteristic: They rev up the action of the central nervous system, increasing energy and improving mood. However, that is the only similarity found in this eclectic group, which includes caffeine, nicotine, and amphetamines, among others. Stimulants vary tremendously in their sources and strengths. Some are extracted from plants, while others are made in a lab. Several are so mildly stimulating that they have few physiological effects; many, however, deliver a serious jolt to the body. But stimulants most differ in how socially acceptable they are.

Regional Favorites

Many of the mild stimulants, such as caffeine, are warmly embraced, appearing at meals and snack time in all corners of the globe. Tea is one of the oldest caffeine-containing beverages in the world. Its use originated in China more than five thousand years ago. Since then it has traveled across the globe, becoming one of the world's most favored beverages.

Coffee is a popular pick-me-up beverage in the United States. The Japanese are serious coffee drinkers, too, and they enjoy other caffeinated drinks that help them stay alert at their desks. In Africa, another form of caffeine is extracted from the kola tree, a plant that is native there. Its caffeine-containing seeds are popular for several reasons. People chew the seeds before meals to make their food easier to digest, use them to garnish their dishes to improve flavor, and add them to foul-tasting water to freshen it. Kola nuts can also be ground up and sprinkled directly on injuries or

Coffee is a popular beverage in many countries. Coffee contains caffeine, one of a group of chemicals known as stimulants that excite the central nervous system.

added to home remedies. In some areas, the seeds are so prized that they can be used as currency.

On a global scale, the production and sales of mild stimulants are major industries. In England alone, consumers enjoy 185 million cups of tea and 75 million cups of coffee a day. To supply caffeinated beverages around the world, thousands of employees raise and process the mildly stimulating plants as well as deliver and serve the products.

Despite the acceptance and wide use of such stimulants around the world, many strong stimulants are used in a more clandestine setting because they lack the approval of society and are illegal in many countries. This latter group includes cocaine and ampheta-

A Bolivian family spreads out coca leaves to dry in the sun. Coca leaves are used to make cocaine, a powerful illegal stimulant.

mines, stimulants that are potentially dangerous. They not only produce adverse effects but also have a great potential for repeated abuse.

A Global Problem

Although the use of mild stimulants raises few concerns, the abuse of strong stimulants is a serious problem. Globally, about 43 million people use some kind of illegal stimulant. During the 1990s, 134 countries reported problems with drug abuse, including the abuse of stimulants. The use of illegal stimulants has negative consequences for the users, their families, and society in general. Some of the costs are financial; society picks up a mammoth tab for care of neglected children, incarceration of drug criminals, and treatment for addiction. However, some of the most severe costs are emotional. Users and their families suffer damage on many levels.

In the past, countries have tried to handle their own drug issues, with varying degrees of success. Now, many countries realize that because stimulant use is so widespread, they must work together to address the issue. The severity of this problem has gained the attention of the UN. At the 1998 session of the United Nations, 188 member countries pledged to help each other significantly reduce the worldwide supply of drugs, as well as the demand for them, by 2008. To make this goal a reality, the UN Office for Drug Control and Crime Prevention (ODCCP) organized a worldwide program that stresses prevention, treatment, and rehabilitation in each country. Globally, the stimulant problem does not appear entirely bleak.

Several countries, including Bolivia, the Lao People's Democratic Republic, Pakistan, Peru, Thailand, and Vietnam, have seen a reduction in the volume of drug trade. In many of the developed countries, drug problems have either slowed or showed a modest decline. In fact, the production of drugs around the globe shows a clear downward trend. This trend is expected to continue as each country, supported by its fellow UN members, embraces the task of putting a stop to the use of illegal stimulants.

Chapter 1

A Brief History
of Stimulants

Today's world is fast paced and demanding. Advertisers send mes-
sages that being thin is fashionable. Parents prod their children
to study hard and earn good grades. Supervisors urge employees to
be more productive. The drive to be the best one can be—thinner,
smarter, or faster—seems to be part of the American psyche.

For those who always feel pressured to achieve more, chemical
stimulants may be appealing. This diverse group of drugs, containing dozens of stimulants, has one common denominator: All of them
speed up the functions of the body, making people feel more alert.
However, stimulants vary widely in how much they accelerate body
activities, the manner in which they are used, and their legal status.

The most commonly used legal stimulants are caffeine and
nicotine, both of which are derived from plants. The best-known
restricted stimulants are cocaine, which also comes from a plant,
and amphetamines, which are synthesized in a lab.

Inside the Body

Although stimulants are derived from several sources, they all alter
the body's functions in about the same way. They change the way
information is carried along nerves.

Throughout the body, nerve cells line up end-to-end to create living superhighways for the transmission of information. Data zips down the length of a nerve in the form of an electrical impulse. However, an electrical impulse cannot travel directly from one nerve cell to the next because there is a small gap, a synapse, located between cells. To get across the gap, the impulse must be ferried by special chemicals called neurotransmitters. So, when an electrical impulse reaches the end of a cell, it stimulates the release of neurotransmitters. These chemicals flow across the synapse, carrying the impulse and stimulating the next cell. In this way, the impulse moves along the chain of nerve cells.

Stimulants do their work at the synapses, where they cause a buildup of neurotransmitters. High levels of neurotransmitters in synapses create several changes in the body. They activate the release of adrenaline, setting off the "fight or flight" response, a system that

Chemicals called neurotransmitters carry electrical impulses between cells (pictured). Stimulants alter body chemistry by increasing the number of neurotransmitters flowing between cells.

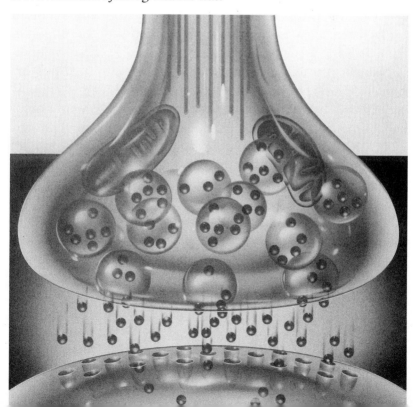

prepares the body for emergencies. Adrenaline increases heart rate, the flow of blood to muscles, and the speed at which impulses are transmitted along nerves. As a result, stimulants make a person feel stronger, more alert, and energized. Some stimulants, like caffeine, only mildly excite the nervous system. Others, like amphetamine, cause very noticeable changes. An adrenaline surge, along with the energy it produces, may not sound harmful. But Andrew Weil and Winifred Rosen, authorities on mind-altering drugs, point out the downside to artificial spikes in adrenaline levels:

> One of life's basic rules is You Never Get Something for Nothing (or, There's No Such Thing as a Free Lunch), and stimulants are no exception to this rule. . . . Instead of miraculously delivering free gifts of cosmic energy, stimulants merely force the body to give up some of its own energy reserves. So when the stimulant wears off, the person feels especially tired, with less than normal energy. This may be perceived as feeling "down," sleepy, or depressed.[1]

The buildup of neurotransmitters at synapses causes another change in the body: It excites a complex brain mechanism called the reward pathway. This pathway is designed to help teach the body to perform tasks required for survival, such as eating, through positive reinforcement.

Nicotine, cocaine, and amphetamines are able to trigger the reward pathway, but they do so in an abnormal way. When consumed, these stimulants do not just switch on the reward system; they overexcite it, causing intense feelings of happiness. The brain quickly learns to associate these feelings with the drugs. Thus, the drugs "teach" the brain that they are essential for survival and that the body cannot manage without them.

The Most Popular Stimulant

Caffeine is the most commonly used stimulant in the world. Because its effects are mild, it does not interact with the reward pathway, but it does speed up the body. About 90 percent of Americans depend on caffeine to jump-start their mornings. This stimulant is found in more than sixty different species of plants

Caffeine is found in more than sixty different species of plants. It is the most commonly used stimulant in the world.

that are used to prepare foods and beverages. Caffeine has played a big part in the development of cultures around the world.

One of the oldest caffeine-containing plants is the coffee tree. Historians believe that the shrubby coffee tree originated in the fourth century B.C. in the area that makes up present-day Ethiopia. From there, traders brought coffee to Venice. By the 1600s, coffeehouses had become popular meeting places where businessmen, scholars, and politicians got together to exchange ideas over a cup of coffee. According to drug historians Cynthia Kuhn, Scott Swartzwelder, and Wilkie Wilson, "The environment created in coffee houses turned out to be one that gave rise to creative thinking in the entrepreneurial and business realms."[2] Coffeehouses spread across Europe and eventually to the young United States.

Even though most people welcomed the spread of coffee across both the Old and New Worlds, some medical experts feared that it was a dangerous brew. In the United States and Europe, doctors hotly debated coffee's safety. A typical cautionary word came from Dr. T.D. Crothers, professor of nervous and mental diseases at the New York School of Clinical Medicine. He taught that coffee was as addicting and dangerous as morphine or alcohol. Describing the downside of coffee addiction, he said, "In some extreme cases, delusional states of a grandiose character appear; rarely violent or destructive, but usually of a reckless, unthinking variety. Associated with these are suspicions of wrong and injustice from others; also extravagant credulity and skepticism."[3] Even today, the medical community has continued to issue occasional warnings to limit coffee's use. Despite these, coffee has remained popular.

Drinking coffee is just one of several ways to consume caffeine. Tea, cola, and chocolate also contain caffeine. Chocolate, the caffeine-containing extract made from the seeds of the cacao plant, has been popular for centuries. About two thousand years ago, the Mayans made a warm, bitter drink from it that they called *chocolatl*; it was so thick that it was eaten with a spoon. Today, most cultures prefer to mix chocolate with sugar to curb the bitter taste.

The Science Behind the Brew

Even though people have been consuming food containing caffeine for centuries, the pure chemical was not identified and isolated until 1821. It is now known that caffeine speeds up the activity of neurons in the brain and causes the release of adrenaline, like other stimulants do. However, caffeine has another action that is less known, one that explains why caffeinated beverages keep people awake at night.

As it works, the brain makes a chemical by-product called adenosine. By the end of the day, adenosine levels in the brain are high. High levels signal to certain cells in the brain that it is time to feel fatigued. Thus, the accumulation of adenosine helps slow the body at the end of the day, preparing it for sleep. Caffeine interferes with this process by blocking the action of adenosine. As a result, cells do not get the signal that it is time to slow down and rest, so they keep working at their normal pace.

Adenosine buildup also signals blood vessels in the brain to dilate. Researchers believe that this dilation helps ensure that plenty of food and oxygen will be delivered to cells during sleep. However, when caffeine is present, the command to dilate does not get sent, so the vessels remain small and constricted.

Caffeine's ability to prevent the dilation of blood vessels in the brain makes it a useful treatment for vascular headaches. Painful vascular headaches are caused by enlarged blood vessels in the brain. Some people who suffer with this condition take prescription caffeine pills when their headaches begin, a strategy that reduces the size of the vessels and prevents the headaches from worsening.

Caffeine also mildly stimulates the nerves that regulate the size of bronchial tubes in the lungs. The stimulation causes these tubes to widen slightly, making it easier to breathe. Researchers are examining this property to see if it may give caffeine some value in treating the sick. For example, in the *Harvard Commentary Health News,* Dr. Robert Shmerling says, "Newborns, especially those who are premature or have undergone surgery just after birth, may be treated with caffeine to stimulate their breathing."[4]

The Leaf of Gold

Following caffeine, nicotine ranks as the second most widely used stimulant. Unlike caffeine, nicotine comes primarily from one source, the leaves of the tobacco plant, *Nicotiana tabacum.* This plant has been tended and harvested for thousands of years.

Tobacco is native to the Americas, and historians have found evidence that it was used as far back as 6000 B.C. When explorer Christopher Columbus and his crew landed on San Salvador island in 1492, the locals offered him gifts of tobacco leaves. In his journal, Columbus wrote, "The natives brought fruit, wooden spears, and certain dried leaves which gave off a distinct fragrance."[5] Imitating the natives, Columbus and his crew smoked and chewed the leaves. Finding tobacco to their liking, they took samples back to Europe to share.

Virginia colonists load tobacco onto ships bound for Europe. Nicotine, the world's second most widely used stimulant, comes from the leaves of the tobacco plant.

By the 1600s tobacco was cultivated in several parts of the United States. In every sense, tobacco was a cash crop that soon became a pillar of American society. According to a nineteenth-century historian,

> So prominent is the place that tobacco occupies in the early records of the middle Southern States, that its cultivation and commercial associations may be said to form the basis of their history. It was the direct source of their wealth, and became for a while the representative of gold and silver; the standard value of other merchantable products; and this tradition was further preserved by the stamping of a tobacco-leaf upon the old continental money used in the Revolution.[6]

Other Uses of Nicotine

While caffeine is usually consumed in food or beverages, nicotine can be introduced into the body by several different routes: through the skin, the membranes lining the mouth and nose, the lungs, or the digestive system. Once nicotine reaches the bloodstream, it travels to the brain within just a few seconds. There, it has many of the same effects as other stimulants: It increases heart rate and blood pressure and activates the reward center of the brain, sending the body the false message that nicotine is necessary for survival.

Examining these properties, scientists think that nicotine may have a role in the treatment of diseases of the brain. Colleen McBride, director of cancer prevention at Duke University, believes that nicotine may have value in treating some of the symptoms of depression, as well as Parkinson's and Alzheimer's diseases, conditions that hamper memory and thinking. According to McBride, "We might put some of these people on nicotine patches or some type of nicotine replacement therapy for life. . . . There's growing evidence that it may be useful in treating Parkinson's disease, Alzheimer's—their level of concentration, their ability to focus."[7]

Amphetamine Arrives

Whereas caffeine and nicotine have been widely used in the Western Hemisphere for centuries, amphetamines are relatively new. Amphetamine was accidentally made in a lab in 1887 by a German scientist working on a treatment for asthma.

Not realizing the potential of his discovery, the scientist put the amphetamine aside and stopped experimentation on it. The drug sat on the shelf for forty years. In 1927 UCLA researcher Gordon Alles decided to explore amphetamine further to see if it had any therapeutic value.

Through experimentation, Alles found that amphetamine is a powerful bronchodilator, which means that it opens the breathing tubes in the lungs. To his surprise, patients who tested the drug told him that it also gave them energy and made them feel good.

Hoping that those stimulating properties were merely unimportant side effects, drug companies put Alles's drug on the market to treat colds and asthma. In the late 1920s, over-the-counter amphetamine inhalers called Benzedrine reached drugstores everywhere. In a short time, the word was out that Benzedrine inhalers not only cleared congestion but delivered a powerful burst of energy. During Prohibition and the depression, periods when very few recreational drugs were available, Benzedrine inhalers were a hit with anyone who wanted a quick buzz. By 1929 drug companies were encouraged by the success of their first amphetamine product and decided to market the drug as a tablet. During World War II, soldiers on both sides of the conflict were given amphetamine tablets to reduce fatigue.

The Birth of Methamphetamine

In the meantime, scientists in Japan were experimenting with the amphetamine molecule to see if it might generate any other potential medicines. One of their experiments yielded methamphetamine, a more potent form of amphetamine. Like its parent drug, methamphetamine could be taken orally. However, because it was a water-soluble powder, it could also be dissolved and injected, providing a more potent way to administer the chemical.

Regardless of how they are consumed, once in the bloodstream, amphetamines travel to the brain in just a few seconds. In the brain tissue, they dramatically increase nerve cell activity, which in turn decreases appetite and causes feelings of energy and excitement. Amphetamines also stimulate the reward center of the brain, delivering strong feelings of pleasure.

With these effects in mind, drug companies enthusiastically marketed amphetamine and its derivatives as treatments for depression and as dieting aids. People in every walk of life found a use for the drugs and a reason to purchase them: Truck drivers who needed to stay awake on long trips, athletes who wanted extra energy, housewives yearning to lose a few pounds, and students cramming for exams sought out the drugs. During each year of the 1950s, manufacturers in the United States produced enough

Candy-Flavored Cigarettes

They come in strawberry, chocolate, vanilla, and grape. Hand rolled and beautifully packaged, flavored cigarettes from India called bidis appeal to many teens. Although they are sometimes marketed as a safe alternative to cigarettes, bidis contain more nicotine than American cigarettes and are loaded with more of the undesirable, cancer-causing ingredient, like tar and other toxins, than traditional cigarettes.

In an interview with the *Ventura County Star*, Dr. Terry Pechacek of the Centers for Disease Control and Prevention's Office of Smoking and Health warns that "These things [bidis] are unregulated, highly available and kids think they're safe. . . . Studies in India find that the lung cancer risk among bidi smokers is higher than people smoking Western style cigarettes."

One state, Illinois, has already taken steps to protect smokers by banning the sale of bidis. "It's a deceptive product," said Senator Kathleen Parker to the *Jefferson City News Tribune*. "It is something they're claiming is going to help a person stop smoking. Actually it's more addictive."

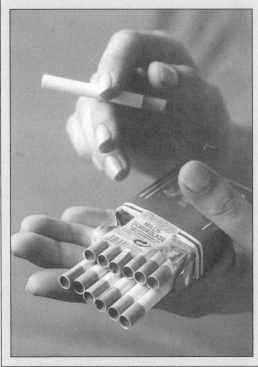

Candy cigarettes, like these chocolates from Germany, contain no nicotine, but candy-flavored bidi cigarettes contain dangerous levels of the stimulant.

amphetamines to supply each man, woman, and child with fifty doses. Most people used them under the recommendation of their physicians.

By 1965 physicians were seeing undeniable signs of addiction in some amphetamine users. Doctors reported these adverse effects to the Food and Drug Administration (FDA) the organization in charge of assuring the safety of foods and drugs used by Americans. As a result, amphetamines were soon placed under federal restrictions to protect consumers.

Today, amphetamines are prescribed to treat patients with ADD, ADHD, or narcolepsy. Here, a boy takes the amphetamine-like drug Ritalin to treat his ADD.

A Role in Medicine

Today there are very few conditions for which physicians prescribe amphetamines. Medical use is restricted to the treatment of attention deficit disorder (ADD) or attention deficit hyperactivity disorder (ADHD) and narcolepsy. ADD and ADHD are characterized by impulsive behavior and disorganized thinking patterns. The most commonly prescribed form of amphetamine for these disorders is Ritalin, chemically known as methylphenidate. Ritalin activates the part of the brain that helps to focus thinking and calm behavior. Narcolepsy is a disorder characterized by an uncontrollable desire for sleep. Narcoleptics may suddenly fall asleep several times during the day, even while talking or driving. The ability of amphetamines to arouse their brains helps them stay awake.

An Interest in Cocaine

Unlike amphetamines, which are made in the lab, cocaine is derived from a natural source. Cocaine is the active ingredient in the leaves of *Erythroxylon coca*, a native plant of South America. Coca cultivation and use by South American cultures dates back to 2500 B.C. when leaves were chewed by the working class to increase their stamina and give them the energy needed to perform physically demanding tasks.

The first Europeans to learn about coca were explorers to the New World. In 1499 Amerigo Vespucci wrote in his journal about the unusual habit of leaf chewing among the South American natives:

> Their cheeks bulged with the leaves of a certain green herb which they chewed like cattle, so that they could hardly speak. . . . When I asked . . . why they carried these leaves in their mouth, which they did not eat, . . . they replied it prevents them from feeling hungry, and gives them great vigor and strength.[8]

Physicians did not seriously consider the drug as a possible medication until 1883. One of the first physicians to do so was an army doctor. According to Edward Brecher, editor of *The Consumers Union Report on Licit and Illicit Drugs*, "German army physician, Dr. Theodor Aschenbrandt, secured a supply of pure

cocaine from the pharmaceutical firm of Merck and issued it to
Bavarian soldiers during their autumn maneuvers. He reported
beneficial effects on their ability to endure fatigue."[9] These results
piqued interest among other physicians and scientists.

The Miracle Cure

Viennese doctor Sigmund Freud, a pioneer in the field of psychology, was intrigued by Aschenbrandt's findings. Edward Brecher
explains:

> Young Freud at the time was suffering from depression, chronic fatigue,
> and other neurotic symptoms. "I have been reading about cocaine," Freud
> wrote to his fiancée in 1884. "I am procuring some myself and will try it
> with cases of heart disease and also of nervous exhaustion."[10]

Following the standard medical protocol of the day, Freud experimented with the drug on himself. He found that a tiny quan-
tity, only one-twentieth of a gram, gave him boundless energy and
relieved his depression. Impressed by these positive results, Freud
tried cocaine on several patients, his sisters, and his fiancée. He
was pleased to find that it seemed to help everyone, no matter
what their condition.

One of Freud's colleagues, German surgeon Carl Koller, was
fascinated by cocaine's ability to act as a local anesthetic, or numb
the skin to which it was applied. As part of his practice, Koller per-
formed eye surgery, an experience that was extremely painful to
his patients. Experimenting with a solution of the white powder
dissolved in water, Koller found that he could deaden the cornea
of a patient's eye. For the first time in history, it was possible to
perform eye surgery without the usual pain. By 1885, Koller's
landmark discovery, along with Freud's continued support and
enthusiasm, generated so much interest in cocaine that doctors,
surgeons, and dentists around the world ordered the drug to try
on their own patients.

In the late 1800s, the medical industry began incorporating
cocaine into hundreds of new elixirs. To sell these products, ad-
vertisements promised that the remedies could cure almost every
known disease. The cocaine-laced Ryno's Hay Fever and Catarrh

Remedy, "for when the nose is stuffed up, red and sore," was also promoted as a tonic that "could make the coward brave, the solent [shy] eloquent, and render the sufferer insensitive to pain."[11] Even Sears, Roebuck, and Company got in the act, offering a Peruvian wine of coca that "sustains and refreshes both the body and brain."[12]

As the world celebrated the many uses of cocaine, a few doctors began to see the drug's ugly side when some patients began to display classic symptoms of addiction. To protect consumers, the federal government ultimately passed the Pure Food and Drug Act which prohibited the use or sale of cocaine without a prescription, in 1906.

In the 1800s cocaine was perceived as a panacea, and was used as an ingredient in hundreds of different pharmaceutical remedies.

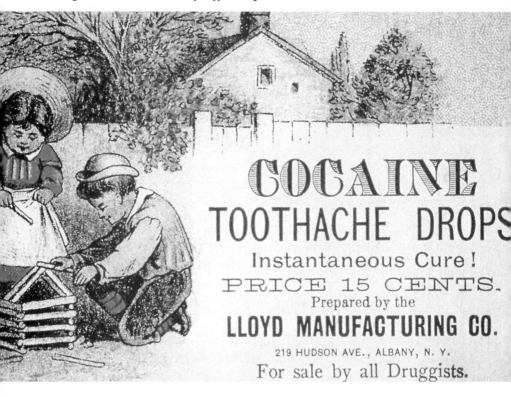

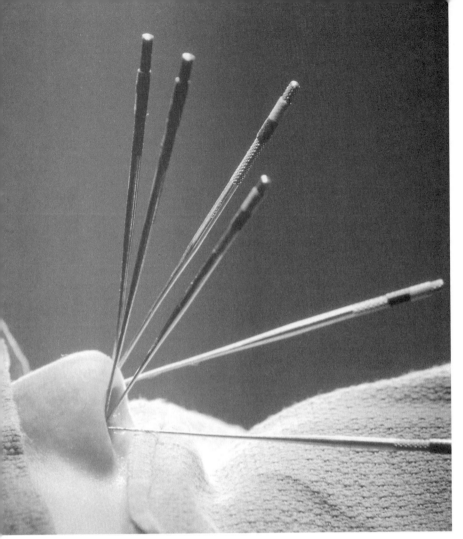

Today cocaine is used as a local anesthetic for surgeries of the eyes, ears, nose, and throat.

Legal Uses Today

As with amphetamines, cocaine's addicting qualities brought it under medical and governmental scrutiny. Working in the same manner as its chemical cousins, cocaine triggers the reward center, creating sensations of intense pleasure. Its mechanism of action, however, is slightly different from the one used by amphetamines, which cause an overproduction of neurotransmitters. Neil Swan, writing for the National Institute on Drug Abuse, explains that cocaine blocks the normal cleanup of neurotransmitters after they are released: "When cocaine is present, it prevents the reabsorption of dopamine [a neurotransmitter]. As a result, the neurotransmitter is left in the synapse of cells in the pleasure center, artificially extending sensations of pleasure."[13]

Today the sale and use of cocaine are even more restricted than they were a century ago, yet cocaine remains an important drug in the operating room. Cocaine is unrivaled as a local anesthetic, used to numb the eyes, ears, nose, and throat during surgery. There are very few other medical uses of the drug. Cocaine is an ingredient in a remedy called Brompton's mixture, which is still sold in Great Britain to alleviate the chronic pain of terminally ill patients. At one time, cocaine was used as a treatment for depression, but substitute medications have been developed that have proved more beneficial.

In the Rhythm

One of the appeals of stimulants is their ability to change the natural rhythms of life, creating energy and alertness on demand. Generally, people are most alert in the mornings, and their energy wanes as the day proceeds. A cola during the afternoon slump can combat drowsiness and fatigue. Used in this way, stimulants are generally safe. However, the use of stronger stimulants is a huge concern for public health and welfare.

Chapter 2

Stimulant Abuse

Although stimulants are the most used drugs in the world, not all of them share the same legal status. Cocaine and most amphetamines have only a few legitimate medical applications; their use for any other reason is forbidden. Methamphetamine is not approved for any type of use. Nevertheless, thousands of recreational users find the appeal of cocaine and amphetamines so strong that they self-administer the drugs in violation of the law.

A Pattern of Abuse

Unfortunately, the federal government's efforts to protect the public from dangerous drugs have not eliminated the problem of stimulant abuse. In the wake of the 1906 ban on nonprescription use of cocaine, cocaine abuse did not disappear. The drug remained popular among thousands of users, and its sales were brisk. Those who elected to keep using it did so in secret to avoid arrest. The public got most of its information about cocaine and its users from wild rumors and sensational stories. As a result, a fear of cocaine users developed in some parts of the country.

Playing into this worry, many newspaper reporters wrote incredible stories about cocaine addicts terrorizing law-abiding citizens. In one 1914 article, Dr. Edward Huntington Williams scared readers across the country with his description of a "cocaine fiend." Williams reported that this violent person was so strong that he could not even be killed with a gun, which is not true. According to the doctor,

> The drug produces an exhilaration . . . that may produce the wildest form of insane excitation, accompanied by the fantastic hallucinations and delusions that characterize acute mania. . . . But the drug produces several other conditions which make the "fiend" a peculiarly dangerous criminal. One of these conditions is a temporary immunity to shock—a resistance to the knockdown effects of fatal wounds. Bullets fired into vital parts, that would drop a sane man in his tracks, fail to check the "fiend"—fail to stop his rush or weaken his attack.[14]

In the late 1920s after amphetamines were introduced, many people were relieved to learn that large numbers of cocaine users were switching to the new drugs. In general, the public believed that amphetamines were safe because they had not been around long enough for people to discover their dangers. Harold E. Doweiko, the author of *Concepts of Chemical Dependency*, explains that the "dangers of cocaine were well known to drug abusers/addicts of the era, but because the long-term effects of the amphetamines were not known, they were viewed as a safe substitute for cocaine."[15]

For the next four decades, the medical community prescribed amphetamines to patients for a variety of ills. However, just as with cocaine, signs of addiction were eventually noted and the drugs were banned. Unfortunately, the pattern of abuse established at the end of the nineteenth century by cocaine was repeated in the last half of the twentieth century by amphetamines. Legislation to regulate the consumption of amphetamines did not deter recreational users; it simply made the drugs more difficult to purchase. Following in the footsteps of cocaine addicts, abusers of amphetamines turned to the black market for their supply of drugs.

The Appeal

There was—and still is—a great demand for cocaine and amphetamines. People who use these chemicals refer to themselves as being "cranked up," "pepped up," "jazzed up," or "hyped." The nicknames for the drugs are self-describing, reflecting either their action or appearance. On the streets, cocaine is known as coke, blow, powder, cane, vitamin C, girl, and crack. Some of the more popular names for amphetamines are speed, crank, powder, ice, tweak, go, uppers, black beauty, pep pills, wake up, and wheels. Methamphetamine is most commonly called meth.

Many young people learn about these substances from friends and acquaintances, and are often introduced to the drugs at parties. Liz is a teen who sometimes attends parties where drugs are common. "You go to parties," she says, "and there will be kids in the bathroom or in a bedroom . . . doing speed and coke."[16]

Why would a young person try amphetamines or cocaine in the first place? People who work with stimulant abusers see three primary reasons. "Curiosity or peer pressure . . . bring them all in,"[17] says Kevin Boender, a counselor who runs a drug abuse program in Idaho. Young people are naturally curious, and many do not fully realize the dangers associated with experimenting with stimulants. Others are pressured by friends who are trying stimulants and feel that they must join in or risk rejection by the group.

Boender also claims that some girls try stimulants because they have heard that the drugs will make them thin. Since these stimulants speed up the body systems and suppress hunger, abusers do not eat much. For some people, the idea of taking stimulants and losing the desire for food sounds more appealing than consciously dieting and wisely planning food choices.

Nancy Echelbarger, who runs Substance Misuse Services in Spokane, Washington, sees many stimulant addicts. She believes that most of her clients are trying to medicate themselves in an effort to avoid dealing with real issues in their lives. According to Echelbarger, "We find no matter what the drug, it is a symptom. Ninety-five percent of both men and women use drugs to cover the memories, pain and anger of a traumatic past, or childhood, or both."[18]

Coca Long Ago

In early Incan society, coca was originally reserved for royalty and priests. Worshippers believed that the coca leaf was a gift from the gods that was given to the first Inca ruler. With the passage of time, common people were permitted to use the leaves as well. They found that they could work longer and harder in their high-altitude homes if they kept a wad of green leaves in their mouths. Each wad was savored for thirty minutes or so and then spit out.

When the Spanish invaded Peru in 1533, they banned the use of coca leaves. To their shock, they found that the natives were no longer able to work long days in the silver mines. As a result, the Spanish soon reversed their position and provided fresh leaves to the Indian laborers during rest breaks. Spaniards who took up the habit of coca-leaf chewing, meanwhile, were viewed as rebels and treated as outcasts. Spanish chewers were forced to leave the colony and live alone or move in with the Indians.

Indian cultures of more recent times worshipped Mama Coca, a goddess who blessed humans with her power. When a worshipper chewed or smoked coca leaves, Mama Coca's power was thought to enter his body. The worshipper believed that this protected his mind and body against any danger. Many present-day natives have similar beliefs and carry out similar practices.

A Big Lift

No matter what motivates a person to try—and continue—using stimulants, these drugs have similar effects on all people. They increase energy, inspiring users to take on a flurry of activity. One young woman remembers how energized she felt when she used amphetamines:

> When I get Crank, I can't wait to get back home and see how I'm going to channel my energy for the next 10 plus hours. Sometimes I write poems or stories. The first time the writing hit me was on the way back from San Francisco. . . . We flew out, then drove back a Brady Bunch Style Station wagon. The drive normally takes 2½ days from [California to South Dakota], but we made it in 28 hours. Wide Awake![19]

Amphetamines and cocaine also generate feelings of confidence. One user, Cynric, and his friend Rob kept "bumping," or repeating

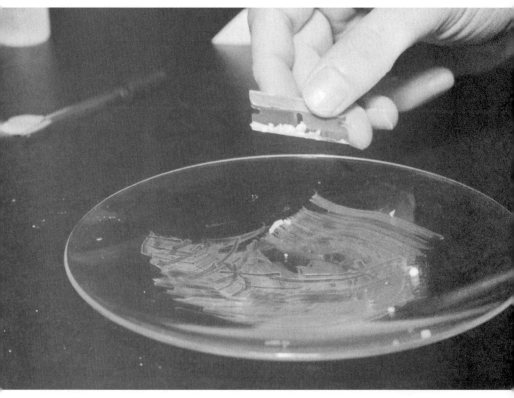

Cocaine and amphetamines are commonly sold as a powder. The powder is snorted through the nose, providing an instantaneous and very powerful high.

hits of meth, to maintain that feeling of confidence for more than thirty hours:

> I felt this incredible feeling . . . like I was king of the world, and I could do anything I wanted. . . . We decided to . . . go to a mountain near my place with lots of hiking trails. . . . When we got to the mountain, we decided to bypass the hiking trails and climb straight up the rock face with no safety harnesses . . . which was also odd because I am afraid of heights. . . . I still have a scar on my leg from where I slammed it into a rock . . . and I didn't even feel it at the time, I just had this attitude like "whatever, I have to get to the top . . . I have to climb!"[20]

In addition to producing a false sense of assurance, meth's effects on the brain can cause an odd and disturbing behavior called getting "hung up." An addict can have the same thought, or carry out the same action, for hours at a time. One person might get hung up cleaning a floor over and over again, another assembling and disassembling a small appliance several times, and still another singing the same song for hours.

Generally, the effects of stimulants are the same no matter how the drugs are ingested. However, the method of use influences how quickly, and how strongly, cocaine and amphetamines affect the body. All are commonly sold as white powders, although meth may occasionally have an off-white or light brown tint. These powders have a strong, chemical odor. They can be swallowed alone or mixed with a beverage or food. Cocaine can also be rubbed on the gums or held under the tongue for absorption though the oral mucus membranes.

Through the Nose

In the powder form, cocaine and amphetamines can also be inhaled. Many users pour their powder of choice onto a mirror, chop it into a fine dust, and sniff it. Inside the nostrils, the drug molecules diffuse across the membranes of the cells and enter the bloodstream. Once blood-borne, they travel quickly to the brain.

The high from snorting cocaine is intense. It begins almost immediately, peaks in fifteen to thirty minutes, and can last a couple of hours. A young woman remembers how she felt after sniffing cocaine: "Everything was brighter; people were warmer. It was an empathic feeling. I was told that I was moving around like a hummingbird for the most part talking a mile a minute."[21]

Many users say that the high from meth lasts much longer than a coke high. First-time users are often surprised to find out that snorting meth gives a high that peaks in twenty minutes, similar to cocaine, but lasts ten hours or more.

Matt Schofield, a reporter for the *Kansas City Star*, asked Denise Byrd, a young meth user, to tell him about her first experience with the drug. Schofield recounts Byrd's story:

> It's early on a Friday night at a friend's weekly poker party. On her right is her host. He bought the drug. . . . Between hands of poker, her host chops at the stuff with a razor blade.

Quickly she inhales . . . making the powder vanish. She grabs her nose. "Never again," she tells herself. "I will never do this again."

Then the high hits. She feels strong. Incredibly strong. So strong that she looks around for something to lift, something heavy. But she feels too wired to think about that for long. Now she wants to talk. "I mean," she tells herself, "this is *the stuff!* This is real."[22]

Slamming Is Serious

Stimulant abusers who want a more intense response from drugs than the one they can get by snorting opt to inject themselves with a needle. This is called slamming. All of the powdered stimulants can be dissolved and injected directly into a vein. The high from injecting is powerful, and it hits immediately, but it is not as long-lived as the high from snorting. Some users compare the instant adrenaline rush from slamming to the feeling one gets while bungee jumping or parachuting.

Injecting stimulants into veins is a dangerous and often difficult process, especially if users have already damaged their veins. Journalist Conrad Evarts interviewed a stimulant addict, identified as Addicta, about her habit of injecting meth under her fingernails and into her neck because the veins of her arms and legs had collapsed. Addicta explains that "It's hard to find my veins. I used to always shoot in my left arm, or my right arm and I can't even hit myself there no more because I've ruined that vein. So under your fingernails is a good place to hit yourself." When Evarts asked how she could get to a vein there, Addicta replied, "I don't know they did it for me, 'cause I couldn't do it for me." She also used her jugular vein:

> I was out here at my friend's house in Nowheresville and my arms were really bad bruised and my friend said, "Well Addicta we can hit you in the neck in your jugular vein." And I said no way. 'Cause all you got to do is do somethin' wrong in that vein and you could die. She had used hers before. Her jugular veins, and my cousins have used theirs. And that's scary though . . . I did [use it]. It didn't matter to me. I just wanted to get high.[23]

Up in Smoke

Stimulant users are continually developing new ways to get drugs into their bodies. Smoking is a relatively recent technique. Because cocaine powder, or cocaine hydrochloride, is very sensitive to heat, it cannot be smoked without first converting it into a different chemical form, which is a very dangerous process,

A drug addict inspects used needles in search of leftover narcotics. Injecting stimulants directly into the veins intensifies the high for many users.

especially for amateur chemists. According to drug abuse expert
Doweiko,

> When cocaine hydrochloride became a popular drug of abuse in the 1970's,
> users quickly discovered that it is not easily smoked. The high temperatures
> needed to vaporize cocaine hydrochloride also destroy it, making it of lim-
> ited value to those who wished to smoke it. Dedicated cocaine abusers of

*Most teens are introduced to illegal substances at parties. Many experiment
with them out of curiosity, as a result of peer pressure, or because of a desire
to be thin.*

the 1970's and 1980's knew that it was possible to smoke the alkaloid base of cocaine; they also knew that transforming cocaine hydrochloride into an alkaloid base was a long, dangerous process. This made the practice of smoking cocaine unpopular before around 1985.[24]

Enterprising drug producers knew that if cocaine could be smoked easily, they could sell more of it. Eventually, they came up with a formula that worked. By heating a mixture of cocaine hydrochloride with a few household chemicals until crystals formed, they created a form of cocaine called crack. The cracking sound the crystals made cooling in the cooking pot inspired the drug's name.

Users heat the crack crystals and inhale the vapors. The intense euphoria, known as a flash high, starts in less than ten seconds and lasts three to five minutes. It is followed by ten or fifteen minutes of milder euphoria. Because the effects wear off so quickly, crack users must repeat doses more often than cocaine users in order to maintain the high.

Since smoking cocaine proved to be popular, few were surprised when a smokable form of meth appeared on the streets in the late 1970s. Called ice or crank, this crystallized meth is a colorless, odorless chip of pure methamphetamine. Crank or ice is to methamphetamine what crack is to cocaine. By heating and inhaling the vapors, crank users receive an instant high that lasts a long time, up to eight hours.

Carlos Perez, a former crank smoker, compares the thrill of crank to the rush associated with scary or exhilarating experiences:

> You feel fabulous because by taking crank your brain becomes super-active, making your whole body feel euphoric and ecstatic. And you feel all this by not doing anything but ingesting the drug. Unlike dropping off the top of a roller coaster or diving from a high cliff into the ocean, where you are consciously aware of what you did to feel that rush.[25]

Treacherous Treats

Meth has one more face, and it is an innocent-looking one: Tablets called *Yaba*, a Thai word meaning "crazy medicine," are becoming increasingly popular in the United States. These brightly colored, sweet-tasting pills are more commonly found in

Kat

Kat, or methcathinone, is a strong stimulant derived from the plant *Cathula edulis*, a native of parts of Africa and Arabia. Kat affects the body in much the same way as amphetamine. In the 1930s and 1940s, pharmaceutical companies tested methcathinone to see if it had any medical uses. It was concluded that the risks and side effects of kat were unacceptable, and further research was abandoned. However, during the research process, scientists learned how to synthesize the drug.

In 1989 a student at the University of Michigan came across the formula for making kat. By 1990, the student began manufacturing the pure extract of kat and selling it in northern Michigan. Its popularity quickly spread to other states.

Kat is now a common street drug. Short-term effects of kat are similar to those of cocaine or meth: increased heart and respiration rates, a sense of euphoria, and increased alertness. Long-term use causes problems much like those brought on by other powerful stimulants, including paranoia, delusions, anxiety, convulsion, and irregular heart rate. After a binge, users often report feelings of severe depression and ideas of suicide.

the western half of the country than anywhere else. Some are small, about one-quarter the size of an aspirin, and can be easily concealed in the end of a straw. Others are larger because they are mixed with caffeine or other stimulants.

The attractive, candylike appearance of these drugs is what appeals to some young people, which worries both former drug users and drug abuse experts. "Candy drugs, of course, I would be on that in a second,"[26] says Alyssa, a seventeen-year-old meth addict.

In an interview with NBC 4 reporters, Alyssa and teenagers Cory and Kerry talked about using meth tablets. Yaba has become Cory and Alyssa's favorite, because as Cory points out, "It's a lot easier to eat a piece of candy than to smoke a pipe [or] sniff a line."[27] He has been abusing Yaba since he was thirteen years old.

Kerry compares the high to snorting meth: "The rush was so intense. I had a broken foot at the time [and] I didn't use the crutches at all that night 'cause I didn't feel anything—it was so amazing. [Sniffing] crystal meth doesn't do anything compared to this."[28]

Bingeing and Crashing

Whether they consume, inhale, or inject the drugs, stimulant abusers often binge, staying high for several days without sleep. They maintain a binge by taking drugs each time their euphoria begins to fade. Bingeing is most common with meth. Meth users, often called tweakers, have been known to stay awake and high for a week or more. Without rest or food, their bodies become worn out and their minds get confused. Steven, a twenty-eight-year-old meth addict, remembers when his habit got out of control:

> My speed use escalated to daily use when I started smoking it. I lost my jobs. Soon I disassociated with my party friends who were weekend users and started running with a new set which consisted of "all the time tweakers," . . . up for 4 days, down for 3 with depression and blackouts for 2 of those 3 days. . . . Most often I was miserable, but I was hooked. I loved speed more at that time than I loved myself.[29]

It seems that all things come at a price, and that philosophy certainly applies to cocaine and amphetamines. After the high, while the body is still processing the drug out of its system, users experience a period often called the "crash." It is most often characterized by sore muscles, exhaustion, and depression. Some users are so sad during the crash that they contemplate, or even commit, suicide.

In his report for the *Kansas City Star*, Matt Schofield recounts Denise Byrd's experiences when her meth began to wear off:

> What Denise and many other novice users don't realize is that meth is a roller coaster ride, and the downside is always just over the next hill. Denise crashes a couple of hours past dawn Saturday, the firestorm in her brain finally out. She wakes just after 4 p.m., way past her usual time for breakfast at Mom's.
>
> Her nose is raw. She rolls her neck. She flops her torso over her legs, hoping a gentle tug on her back muscles will ease the soreness. She caresses her feet, trying to massage out the knots. Her muscles had been tense, quivering, tingling, throughout the high. Now she feels as if she has run a marathon and then been in a prize fight.
>
> "Who beat me up?" she wonders momentarily, before remembering the meth.
>
> All this from a 2-inch line? But banging around in her brain like a kid with a toy drum is the thought: "More. You want more of that. You need more of that."[30]

Kerry, a teen user, points out that although he loves the high, he hates meth when the high comes crashing down: "You feel really nasty. . . . I mean your bones start to ache, it starts to rot your teeth. It's evil, pretty much, the way it made me feel is just like pure evil." Alyssa, another teen, adds, "Your hair becomes very greasy. Acne, white face, dilated eyes, your fingernails will be ex-

A Colombian man pours gasoline over coca leaves to make coca paste. The paste is later converted into crystallized cocaine, a smokable form of the drug known as crack.

tremely dirty under them. You cannot hide them. You can take a million showers, they will be dirty. You sweat a lot. You're impatient, you're frustrated."[31]

The Products of Time

In the nineteenth century, scientists extracted the active ingredient from the natural stimulant coca, making cocaine available in a concentrated form. Fifty years later, work on another natural stimulant led to the synthesis of amphetamines, producing another powerful drug. This alchemy has dramatically changed the roles that some stimulants play by creating potent, highly desirable drugs of abuse. Today people often find that the continued use of such drugs causes serious problems.

 **Chapter 3**

Dangers of Stimulant Addiction

Illegal stimulants are prevalent drugs of abuse. According to the 2001 National Household Survey on Drug Abuse, the number of people trying illegal stimulants for the first time tripled between 1991 and 2000. Worse, many of these people continued to use drugs. For example, the office of National Drug Control Policy says that in 2001 there were almost 2 million occasional cocaine users and an additional 1.7 million people who used the drug on a regular basis. Though all stimulants have the potential for misuse, nicotine, cocaine, and amphetamines are the most commonly abused and the most dangerous. Long-term usage of any of the three can seriously damage the heart, blood vessels, and lungs and lead to prolonged illness. These drugs are also the most addictive stimulants.

The ABCs of Addiction

Addiction is a condition in which a person compulsively uses a substance, or repeats a behavior, even though it has negative consequences. The term *addiction* comes from a Latin word that means "binding to something." This definition paints a vivid picture of the relationship some people develop with stimulants. The bond can be powerful and difficult to break.

An experienced twenty-eight-year-old drug user puts her own blunt spin on the word *addict*. She and some of her best friends have been addicted to stimulants. "Addicts . . . completely lack self-control," she says. "The drug controls them, they don't control the drug."[32]

Addiction is characterized by compulsive drug use despite the consequences. Nicotine, cocaine, and amphetamines are the most commonly abused drugs.

Why would people let themselves be "controlled" by a stimulant? No one expects to become an addict; addiction usually evolves along a path of increasing use. Paul Gahlinger, author of *Illegal Drugs*, explains: "Illegal drug use can be considered to fall into one of the following categories, where any level . . . may progress to the next: Experimental, Recreational, Circumstantial, and Compulsive."[33]

Escalating Use

A person may experiment with illegal stimulants for many reasons. He may want to know how a drug will make him feel or be urged by friends to try it. Rachel Tope had heard about drugs since middle

The Addiction Theory

How does a person become addicted to stimulants? Dr. Alan Leshner, writing for the National Institute on Drug Abuse, explains his theory.

It is an all-too-common scenario: A person experiments with an addictive drug like cocaine. Perhaps he intends to try it just once, for "the experience" of it. It turns out, though, that he enjoys the drug's euphoric effect so much that in ensuing weeks and months he uses it again—and again. But in due time, he decides he really should quit. He knows that despite the incomparable short-term high he gets from using cocaine, the long-term consequences of its use are perilous. So he vows to stop using it. His brain, however, has a different agenda. It now demands cocaine. While his rational mind knows full well that he shouldn't use it again, his brain overrides such warnings. Unbeknown to him, repeated use of cocaine has brought about dramatic changes in both the structure and function of his brain. In fact, if he'd known the danger signs for which to be on the lookout, he would have realized that the euphoric effect derived from cocaine use is itself a sure sign that the drug is inducing a change in the brain—just as he would have known that as time passes, and the drug is used with increasing regularity, this change becomes more pronounced, and indelible, until finally his brain has become addicted to the drug.

And so, despite his heartfelt vow never again to use cocaine, he continues using it. Again and again. His drug use is now beyond his control. It is compulsive. He is addicted. While this turn of events is a shock to the drug user, it is no surprise at all to researchers who study the effects of addictive drugs. To them, it is a predictable outcome.

school, and by the time she was a high school freshman, she estimated that 75 percent of her friends had experimented with them. Rachel says, "I was curious. It was what all my friends were doing."[34]

Experimenting with strong stimulants can lead to the next phase, recreational use. According to Gahlinger, recreational users sometimes take drugs when they get together with friends. At this stage, illegal stimulant users see the drugs as a way to change their mood or to increase the enjoyment of a social situation.

For some people, part-time, recreational drug use can escalate to the more dangerous phase of circumstantial use. Nicole Hansen, Miss Teen Utah in 2001, was amazed when she realized that she had become a compulsive abuser within just a few months of first trying illegal stimulants. Nicole remembers, "I started popping [injecting under the skin] every other Saturday night. It was fun going to parties and meeting new people. Soon I was using every Thursday, Friday and Saturday."[35]

Circumstantial users like Nicole find themselves turning to illegal stimulants more than they had originally planned. As a result, performance at school and work may decline, and their behavior may seem out of character to others. They try to hide their use, keeping the secret from family, employers, and friends at school. As Lyn, a former stimulant abuser, says, "All of a sudden, you have so many secrets to keep from others, so many lies to hide from your friends."[36] The ongoing deception often alienates users from people who were once close, resulting in feelings of aloneness and depression.

When a person can no longer resist the emotional and physical desire for stimulants, compulsive use or addiction has set in. At this point, the drug dictates every aspect of life. After taking drugs for so long and becoming so dependent on them, many addicts cannot function in any capacity without stimulants. Their lives can spiral out of control, leading to problems with their health, their family, their school and work, or the law.

The Cause of Withdrawal

No formula or timetable can predict if an abuser will become an addict, or how long it will take for addiction to develop. The degree to which stimulants cause addiction varies with the drug of choice and with the user. However, all addicts experience the same basic components of habitual use, no matter which stimulant they prefer.

When a person starts using stimulants, cells throughout the body respond to the drugs as they would to any other foreign material: They try to function normally by working around them. However, if the chemicals keep reappearing, cells eventually accept them as part of a new norm. Cells then adjust to the drugs by moderating their reactions to the stimulants. This causes tolerance, a reduced response when exposed to the drug.

Stimulant addicts develop two types of tolerance: physical and psychological. As physical tolerance builds, addicts find that they must use increasingly larger doses of the drug to feel high. When stimulants are not available, uncomfortable physical symptoms occur; this is known as physical withdrawal. In stimulant addiction, physical withdrawal includes a few days of flu-like symptoms.

Psychological Tolerance

Although physical withdrawal from stimulants is moderate in comparison to withdrawal from other drugs, stimulants' powerful interaction with the reward center of the brain causes severe psychological tolerance. Cells in the reward center realize that the flood of neurotransmitters and the strong surges of electrical impulses that occur with stimulant use are abnormal brain activities. The brain tries to protect itself from these overloads by slowing down the number and frequency of impulses. It cuts back on the number of nerve cell receptors that are available to pick up the impulses, assuring that only a portion of the impulses will be relayed.

This cutback strategy tones down sensory input in the short run, but it causes other problems. With fewer receptors functioning, addicts find that the small doses they used early in their drug experience no longer produce the mind-blowing highs that made the drug attractive in the first place. To compensate, they increase

Deprived of its regular supply of stimulants, the addict's body exhibits severe symptoms of pain and discomfort, known as physical withdrawal.

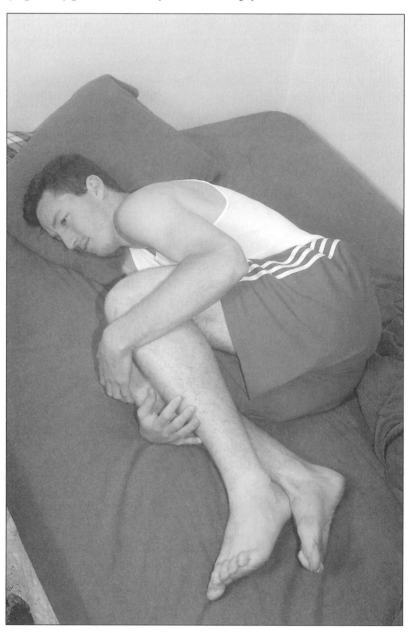

their dosage. In the case of cocaine and amphetamines, users may triple their dosage in just a few weeks.

In the long run, tolerant cells become so habituated to the presence of the drug that they cannot operate normally without them. At that point, when the brain is deprived of stimulants, the reward center goes back to depending on normal levels of neurotransmitters for pleasure. Unfortunately, with fewer receptors in action, normal levels are too low to produce any feelings of happiness, satisfaction, or pleasure. As a result, the person feels tired, depressed, and discouraged, a condition called psychological or emotional withdrawal. As Kuhn, Swartzwelder, and Wilson explain, "Once the drug is gone, the few receptors left are not enough to do the job . . . so the cure has become the disease."[37]

As a result of both physical and psychological tolerance, a user who stops taking stimulants experiences a tidal wave of bad feelings. Only two things can end these withdrawal symptoms: another dose of stimulants or time. Given enough time, the body will recover from most of the changes caused by earlier stimulant use. But it can be tough for a nicotine, cocaine, or amphetamine addict to give the body the time it needs to repair damage. Some who have experienced withdrawal in the past are anxious to avoid it again, so they continually use drugs to stay away from those bad feelings. At this stage, they are tangled in a vicious cycle that seems to have no end.

Who Uses Nicotine?

Of the three strongly addictive stimulants, nicotine is the most widely used. The 2001 National Household Survey on Drug Abuse identified about 66.5 million tobacco (and therefore nicotine) users in the United States. The majority are young adults between the ages of eighteen and twenty-five. However, the fastest growing segment of the tobacco-using population is the twelve- to seventeen-year-olds. The majority of nicotine users smoke—cigarettes, cigars, or pipes—while others chew tobacco.

Most of the 66.5 million individuals who smoke say that they would like to stop. Why don't they? They cannot easily quit because they are addicted, claim the authors of *Drugs and Society*.

These experts explain that "the inevitability of cigarette addiction is undisputable. Studies have shown that 70% of current smokers want to quit but cannot."[38]

When people who smoke or chew tobacco do stop, they experience many withdrawal symptoms. People trying to separate their lives from nicotine must endure cravings, irritability, restlessness, insomnia, aches, anxiety, and impaired judgment. These troublesome symptoms, which start just hours after the last tobacco use and can continue for months, are the primary reason most people go back to using nicotine.

Dangers of Nicotine

Most tobacco users are aware of the damage it can do to their health. Death is the most drastic result. According to the surgeon general, "Cigarette smoking is the single most preventable cause of premature death in the United States. Each year, more than 400,000 Americans die from cigarette smoking. In fact, one in every five deaths in the United States is smoking related."[39]

The majority of these deaths are caused by cancer. Tobacco use is the primary cause of cancers of the lung, mouth, throat, pancreas, uterus, kidney, and bladder. It is also a major factor in a host of other debilitating conditions, such as emphysema, asthma, pneumonia, heart disease, high blood pressure, and stroke.

Impact on Nonsmokers

Sometimes, even those who do not smoke experience the negative consequences of nicotine use. Almost 20 percent of pregnant women ages fifteen to forty-four are smokers. Smoking during pregnancy has serious implications for the fetus. When a pregnant woman smokes, high levels of carbon monoxide (a poisonous gas) and nicotine enter her body, then cross the placenta to reach the fetus. There, these two dangerous chemicals may become fifteen times more concentrated in the fetal blood supply than they are in the mother's blood. These toxins interfere with the baby's ability to receive and use oxygen.

As a result, women who smoke have an increased risk of spontaneous abortion, or loss of the fetus. Babies born to smoking

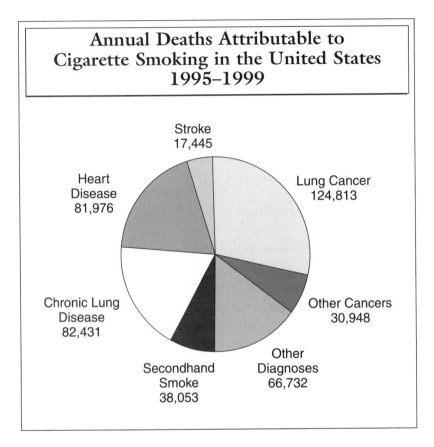

Annual Deaths Attributable to Cigarette Smoking in the United States 1995–1999

Stroke
17,445

Heart
Disease
81,976

Lung Cancer
124,813

Chronic Lung
Disease
82,431

Other Cancers
30,948

Secondhand
Smoke
38,053

Other
Diagnoses
66,732

mothers are more likely to have breathing conditions such as asthma than those born to nonsmokers. They also have an increased risk of premature delivery and low birth weight. Research has shown that the more a mother smokes, the greater the reductions in her child's birth weight. Women who stop smoking early in their pregnancy generally deliver babies with the same birth weights as babies of nonsmokers.

In addition to harming unborn babies, exposure to tobacco smoke is dangerous to children. Secondhand smoke comes from two sources: the end of a burning cigarette and the exhaled breath of a smoker. The American Lung Association reports that people who breathe secondhand smoke are exposed to four thousand chemicals, forty-three of which are known to cause cancer. Even though secondhand smoke is dangerous for people of all ages, small children are more vulnerable than adults, and therefore more likely to suffer long-term health problems.

Who Uses Coke and Meth?

Like smokers, cocaine and meth users are a large and diverse crowd whose numbers are growing. According to the National Household Survey on Drug Abuse, between 1994 and 2000, the last year for which statistics are available, first-time users of illegal stimulants increased from 219,000 to 697,000. In this time period, the number of new users in the age group from twelve to seventeen years was significantly larger than in the age group from eighteen to twenty-five years. Cocaine is the second most commonly used illegal drug in the United States, with meth close behind it. In 2000, the office of National Drug Control Policy reported that 445,000 people frequently used cocaine and 356,000 frequently used meth.

The Cost to Mind and Body

Use of illegal stimulants, especially long-term use, affects both the body and the mind. Because illegal stimulants decrease appetite, and since addicts spend much of their money on drugs rather than food, many users do not eat enough to support their daily caloric needs. Combined with lack of sleep, this causes excessive wear and tear to their bodies.

To make matters worse, prolonged use of these drugs can cause longer-lasting conditions. Many meth addicts look twice their age because of the physical trauma of repeated binges. Sky, a former addict, regrets the toll that bingeing took on her body:

> During the last few months of my overpowering addiction I had lost about seven sizes. . . . I had translucent skin, bloody scabs and pick marks all over my body, my kidneys were failing, brittle hair and nails, paranoia, hallucinations, phobic and panic problems, weak muscles and a very low immune system to fighting off sickness. Actually, the . . . problems that I had . . . are too many to list.[40]

Reporter Ken Olsen learned about what causes these problems from Dr. Thomas Martin, director of the University of Washington's Toxicology Service. Olsen relayed, "Meth addicts don't eat and don't sleep, sometimes for a month. All of their body's resources go to maintaining the high. There's no energy for normal tissue repair. . . . Gums break down. Teeth fall out. Major organs such as the kidneys disintegrate. Sores don't heal."[41]

Some users, especially those who repeatedly use stimulants, develop paranoid or hostile attitudes. One young man who has been on meth since 1996 often runs outside the house, where he lives with his mom, armed with knives and ready to fight. His mother explains that "he thinks people are after him."[42] Even worse, this paranoia may persist long after the drugs are out of the body. Another man, clean for five years, still props heavy objects against doors when he enters a room because he is afraid that someone might be after him.

Such hostility and paranoia are not unusual in stimulant addicts, especially those on meth. Heavy users may hear and see things that are not really there. T.M., a meth addict in treatment, recalls the visions he had after a three-day binge: "I would see what looked like patches of smoke or mist. It seemed there was a person lurking in every shadow, the shadow people. I would hear voices and see things that weren't there. The voices were faint whispers plotting against me."[43]

Under the Skin

Those who binge may also experience formication, the unpleasant feeling that insects are crawling under their skin. This eerie sensation causes bingers to pick at their skin, leaving bloody, open sores that usually need medical treatment. Among users, this problem is known as crank bugs, meth mites, or coke bugs. Fifteen-year-old Tina, who is now clean and living in Austin, Minnesota, saw the work of the "mites" firsthand:

> There was this kid who had been up for like two or three weeks straight and he was picking at his nose because he thought there were bugs crawl-

ing around in there. He picked these big, bloody holes in his nostrils, and he finally took a scissors and cut into his nostrils on both sides.[44]

Dr. Steven O'Mara, an emergency room physician at the Northwest Medical Center in Springdale, Arkansas, sees "bugs" and "mites" all too often. "We have lots of people who come in here who are literally scarred," O'Mara says. "They'll come in and they'll be scratching, picking 'bugs' off themselves. . . . They literally claw themselves."[45]

Bugs, visions, paranoia, and weight loss are just some of the problems caused by the excessive use of coke or meth. The long-term complications to the body are more complex and dangerous, including such things as heart disease, stroke, and permanent damage to brain cells.

Long-term stimulant use is damaging to the body. These photos document how four years of methamphetamine use dramatically transformed a woman's appearance.

1998   **2002**

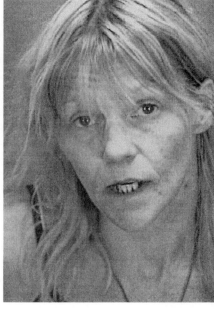

Out of Touch with Reality

In 1938 the first case of amphetamine psychosis, permanent paranoia resulting from amphetamine use, was reported. The psychosis began as a vague feeling of suspiciousness. As it got worse, the amphetamine user began to believe that everything around him related to him in some way. Listening to a newscast, he thought that every bit of information, from reports of plane crashes to local football scores, had special relevance to him. Eventually, severe delusions developed, and the user became paranoid, believing that everyone was his enemy.

Over the Long Haul

One of the most serious complications of stimulant abuse is damage to the heart and blood vessels. Since stimulants rapidly accelerate the heart rate while simultaneously constricting blood vessels, making them work harder, they can weaken the cardiovascular system. Young adults rarely suffer from the same kinds of cardiovascular problems that cause heart attacks in older adults. Consequently, when a young person does experience heart damage, medical personnel always check to see if illegal stimulants are involved. Hospitals report that cocaine is cited most often in young heart damage.

Those who take illegal stimulants may also experience seizures as a result of damage to their brain and other parts of their nervous system. After three years of daily cocaine use, an anonymous addict gave this candid description of herself: "The cocaine was beginning to affect my central nervous system, where I would twitch. . . . I would have seizures and convulsions from doing too much."[46]

Besides causing convulsions, cocaine and meth use can result in permanent brain damage. In a recent study at Yale University, researchers found that a cocaine addict's response to stimulation is reduced, a symptom that may indicate permanent damage. Nashaat Boutros, the principal investigator of the study, says,

> Contrary to what we expected, the results showed that cocaine-dependent individuals displayed increased resistance to brain stimulation. We expected them to be jumpy or more responsive because of the sensitizing effects of cocaine, but it took much stronger stimulation to get them to respond.[47]

Special Problems for Meth Users

Some doctors have been surprised to see young patients displaying symptoms associated with diseases of aging, like Parkinson's and Alzheimer's. These patients were all meth users, and meth has been found to damage the brain in ways similar to those diseases, interfering with memory and learning. Jack Whittkopp, the program director for chemical dependency services at Austin Medical Center, says,

> This drug [meth] ages the brain significantly, and we're only now starting to see studies that suggest the scale of the problems down the road. You see 19 year olds with depleted dopamine [neurotransmitter] levels that you generally associate with people who are 59. We could potentially be looking at a whole bunch of cases of early-onset Alzheimer's and Parkinson's and all sorts of other neurological complications. The horrible thing, of course, is that you're not supposed to experience this kind of neurological damage until you're aged.[48]

Additional Damage

Many addicts also suffer from problems that are distinctive to their method of use. The techniques of injecting, smoking, and snorting create their own unique complications. For those who inject stimulants, the regular use of a hypodermic needle can damage blood vessels and therefore restrict the flow of blood. Blood flow can be further impeded by contaminants in the drugs that clog vessels, resulting in damage to tissues and organs that have been cut off from their normal blood supply. In addition, sharing needles carries a high risk of contracting blood-borne diseases such as HIV, hepatitis B, and hepatitis C.

Snorting and smoking are not benign, either. People who inhale cocaine or meth eventually damage the cells that make up the nasal lining, causing a constant runny nose. Extreme use can even erode or eat away portions of the septum, the structure that separates the nostrils. Smoking, meanwhile, leads to an increased incidence of breathing problems, a chronic cough, chest pain, and damage to lungs.

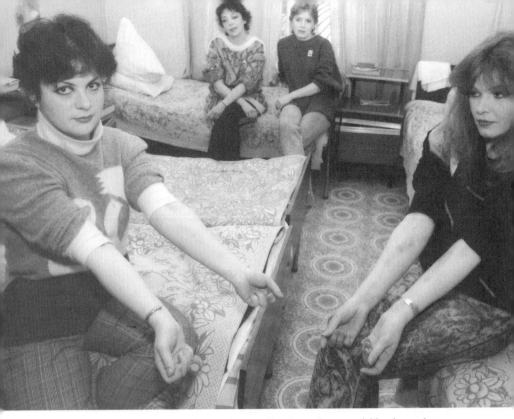

Addicts who inject stimulants often suffer from damaged blood vessels, bruises, and needle marks on their forearms.

The Ultimate Price

A large dose of any illegal stimulant, whether taken purposely or accidentally, can send a user straight to the emergency room, or the morgue. A coke addict recalls how he accidentally overdosed on an unusually pure, and potent, batch of cocaine:

> It is pure terror. Quite simply it feels like you are in the beginning stages of a heart attack and "the lights are about to go out" on your life at any moment. Your heart is beating so rapidly it becomes impossible to take your pulse. The fear shoots more adrenaline into your system, which just makes everything worse. I cannot think of a worse way to die.[49]

A comprehensive study by the National Institute on Drug Abuse found that death from cocaine overdose occurs at a rate of about eight per one hundred thousand people who use the drug. According to one physician, "Sudden death is the most serious result of cocaine abuse. It can be due to a series of savage convulsions, paralysis of the breathing, or sudden heart failure."[50] The rate of overdose increases dramatically when cocaine is mixed with other drugs. Research from Austria indicates that the rate of non-fatal overdose is about seven times higher in people who combine cocaine with other drugs.

Injured Babies

Abusers and addicts are not the only victims of coke and meth; many others are hurt by the drug, too. Pregnant women taking illegal stimulants risk serious health problems, or even the death, of their unborn. The drugs can kill an unborn baby or cause a stroke, which triggers brain damage. During pregnancy, the use of illegal stimulants reduces the amount of nutrients and oxygen that reach the baby, so babies born to abusers are smaller and less healthy than those of women who do not use stimulants.

When Ken Olsen interviewed Lindy Haunschild, coordinator of the Parent-Child Assistance Program in Spokane, Washington,

Pregnant addicts often give birth prematurely to underweight babies with serious health problems.

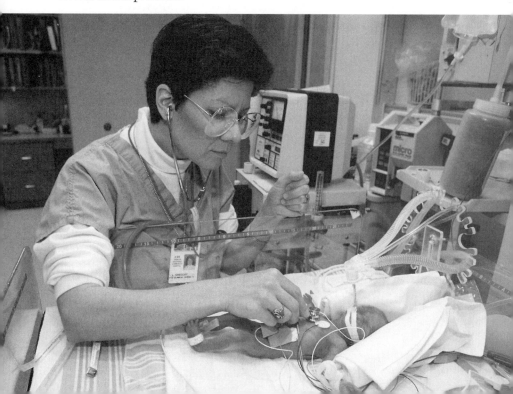

he learned about babies who were born addicted to meth. Olsen found out that if women used meth while pregnant, their babies were born "with behavioral problems and tremors, and they scream from withdrawal 24 hours a day. Many grow up to be users themselves because [according to Haunschild] 'their systems are hard-wired to crave this drug.'"[51]

Olsen also talked to Angela, a meth addict in treatment. Her baby is due in a few months. He wrote,

> Her child will have an operation almost immediately after it's born. Otherwise, the baby would die within a few days. An ultrasound shows the infant's heart is backward and has two holes. That's a condition nicknamed "worm heart." Officially it's called "transposition of the great vessels" and it's another signature of meth.

Olsen learned that during normal development, a child's heart will rotate into the correct position. However, "when the mom is a meth addict, the heart often remains reversed."[52]

Meth hinders the development of other organs as well. Dr. Alex Stalcup, the medical director of New Leaf Treatment Center in Concord, California, explained to Olsen, "The brain, heart and kidneys form very early on—often before the mom knows she is pregnant—when the developing baby is the size of your thumb. If there's an insult to the organs, they don't develop properly. Meth is a very serious insult."[53]

Children in Danger

Babies are not the only casualties of stimulant abuse. When a person is hooked on meth or cocaine, the entire family suffers, especially children. Teri Jones, a caseworker for child welfare, tells reporter Jon Bonné that half her cases are children whose meth-using parents either did not notice or did not care that their children were sick or in danger. Jones's files

> detail the drug's toll on kids born to a meth-using mother or those living around its manufacture: children with respiratory infections, unable to gain weight, absorb nutrients or have normal bowel movements. . . . An infant was found crawling among spilled acids . . . near Newport. . . . The boy had second-degree burns on his knees and palms.

Addicted parents often neglect their children. This inattention can result in significant physical, mental, and emotional problems for the children.

But what may take a most lasting toll on the children is the severe, chronic
neglect. Social workers say it is not uncommon to find 8-year-olds who've
never been to school. Social workers often find older, "parentified" children who bathe, feed and care for younger siblings.[54]

When a person becomes addicted to stimulants, the entire family suffers. If the chronic user loses a job, the family can be left
without a home, a car, or food. Many addicts, in need of quick
cash, turn to crime, a decision that can result in their arrest and
imprisonment. In addition, child welfare agencies are often called
in to take the children of stimulant abusers into protective custody.

Ladeeta Smith, a Brooklyn girl, knows all too well how a
cocaine-using mother can impact a family. Ladeeta and her sisters
had to move in with their grandmother after their mother was arrested for cocaine possession. While in prison, Ladeeta's mother
learned that she had become infected with HIV. She died in jail at
the age of thirty-nine, leaving three children to be raised by their
grandmother.

In the End

In the final analysis, illegal stimulants fall short of most users' ex-
pectations. Whether one is seeking a way to lose weight, be more
productive, or just have fun, the end result is often addiction and
long-term health problems. Researchers are learning more each
year about the long-term effects of stimulants, especially methamphetamine, and some of the most recent findings are alarming.
Their insights into how strong stimulants act on the body have
prompted others to reevaluate the traditional methods for treating and caring for stimulant addicts.

Treatment for Stimulant Addiction

In the United States, experts estimate that stimulant abuse costs citizens about $43,000 a year for each addict who steals, receives welfare after losing a job, forfeits his or her children to custody of the state, or goes to jail. On the other hand, it costs about $16,000 to provide the best treatment available for that same addict. For most, treatment is the only way back to responsible living.

The Nicotine Trap

The number of people addicted to nicotine, one out of three Americans, is much greater than the total of both cocaine and amphetamine addicts. Surveys conducted by the American Lung Association found that 70 percent of nicotine users say they would like to quit. However, nicotine is a tough drug to walk away from. One regretful smoker put it this way: "In a London subway, I once saw a sign that said, 'Addiction to nicotine is worse than addiction to heroin.' At the time I first read this sign, I thought it was a complete exaggeration. But now, eight years later, I am convinced it's true."[55]

Dinah, a smoker for twenty-two years, recalls the difficulty she had in quitting. She describes her experience:

Patients pray at a drug rehabilitation center. Many users enter substance abuse centers or programs to help them overcome their addiction.

I tried to quit "Gracefully," there was nothing graceful about it, besides the "miracle of Grace" in actually quitting. I fought tooth and nail against cravings, bad attitude, and anxiety. Every single morning I would have to decide whether or not to smoke that minute, that hour, that day. My mind would pop the question, "Time for a smoke?" It was horrible.[56]

Even the rituals associated with smoking make the goal of quitting a very tough one to achieve. Studies show that the hand-to-mouth motion is comforting to smokers. In fact, 80 percent of ex-smokers surveyed said that they were always looking for something to pick up and put in their mouths. Similar conclusions were reached in a survey by the American Lung Association, which found that smokers who want to stop really miss "having something to hold in [their] fingers."[57]

When Being a Quitter Is Good

Most smokers try to quit at least once a year. Many are not successful on their first try; on average, it takes more than five attempts to stop smoking for good. Seventeen-year-old Amanda tried several times before she quit. She says,

> In the beginning of the year I had a smoking habit. It was very hard to stop and it took me three tries. (Even with the help of my mom, my teacher, and my friends.) Smoking may seem cool and fun but it's not. My 7-year-old brother wants to smoke because I did. It's hard for him to understand that it's a bad thing and that it hurts you.[58]

Few people quit cold turkey, or stop abruptly, without help. Most need a tailor-made, step-by-step plan. The American Lung Association has created a "Quit Smoking Action Plan" that lets smokers pick a strategy that works for them. The plan suggests setting a target date on which to completely stop smoking. Writing the date on a calendar and telling one or two good friends about the plan also helps; friends can provide emotional support. On the night before the target date arrives, smokers should get rid of all tobacco and tobacco accessories, like lighters, matches, and ashtrays.

The American Lung Association also advises that it is easier to carry out the strategy at a time when life stressors are minimal; that way, the plan can receive top priority for three to four weeks. The best plans are those that include several actions, each designed to reinforce the other. Smokers are encouraged to make a list of all the reasons it is important to stop smoking, and to carry that list in a pocket or purse. It also helps to stay away from other smokers and from places where smoking seems natural. This may require a change in daily habits. For example, if smoking after dinner was a habit, then the usual routine could be changed so that the time after dinner is spent on a stroll outdoors instead.

Some research shows that if cessation is gradual, withdrawal symptoms are not as severe, and nicotine addicts are more likely to stick with their plan. To taper off nicotine gradually, some people benefit from pharmacological help such as nicotine gum and patches. Nicotine patches introduce a small amount of nicotine to

Many people find over-the-counter products such as nicotine patches or gum helpful in their efforts to stop smoking.

the body over a period of several hours. For those who need more help, counseling and support groups, hypnosis, acupuncture, or some antidepressant medications may be useful.

It is possible to quit smoking, and people do it every day. With time, effort, and a little help from friends, they conquer the habit and feel more in control of their lives and futures.

Opting for Treatment

During the 1970s most people believed there were few, if any, dangers associated with either legal or illegal stimulants. When cocaine use peaked in the 1980s and 1990s, addicts flooded the medical community with requests for help and treatment, presenting a new problem for practitioners. Very few members of the medical and counseling communities had seen or treated cocaine addiction before. Thus, few treatment plans or centers existed for cocaine addiction.

By the 1980s physicians and counselors knew a little about how cocaine and amphetamines affect the body. As a variety of strategies came and went, doctors learned what works and what does not work in the way of treatment. One of the oldest drug treatment centers is San Francisco's Haight Ashbury Free Medical Clinic. Started in 1967 by Dr. David Smith, the clinic originally opened its doors to treat drug users during a summer festival. Today the clinic has expanded its services to include both immediate medical care and a residential recovery program that treats cocaine and methamphetamine addicts.

At the Haight clinic, and in other stimulant abuse treatment centers around the United States, the goals are to help addicts give up drugs, learn to cope with their problems, and rebuild their lives. Clients are usually involved in months, or even years, of work. For the first six months, most undergo very intense treatment. After that, follow-up counseling can last for years.

The success of treatment depends on the willingness of the addict to overcome his or her problem. In other words, to be successful, an addict must be motivated to get better. K.R. is a young man who used stimulants heavily. He decided to quit after losing forty-five pounds in four months due to drug use. With the help of counselors, K.R. says, "I went through about 1 month of withdraws. . . . Now I want to get my life straight and there is absolutely no room for speed in my life. . . . I consider doing speed the biggest mistake of my life."[59]

Unlike K.R., many illegal stimulant addicts do not enter treatment voluntarily. According to research conducted by the Koch Crime Institute,

> Methamphetamine causes a variety of mental, physical and social problems which may prompt entry into treatment. . . . The most commonly reported reason why methamphetamine users enter treatment is trouble with the law. These legal problems include aggressive or bizarre behaviors which prompt others to call police. Other reasons for entry include mental or emotional problems and problems at work or at school.[60]

Counselors have found that the best time to talk to addicts about voluntary treatment is when they are coming down from the thrill and euphoria of their last stimulant rush. Says John DiDomenico, supervisor of the Haight Ashbury clinic, "Nobody wants to face the crash. It's real easy to grab them at that point."[61] The crash can be such a difficult and scary experience that users who previously did not want to quit often see the value of help.

Starting with a Clean Slate

All treatment programs begin with detoxification, sometimes known as detox. Detox refers to the period of time during which the body eliminates all of the drugs in its system. It is an essential step in recovery, because all traces of the drug must be removed from tissues of the brain and body before they can completely heal.

When they enter treatment, coke and meth users may be physically run-down. During detox they need a safe place to sleep for several days so that their bodies can start recovering from exhaustion. Many users receive care for problems like rotting teeth, infected skin, or infectious diseases.

During detox, people undergo both physical and mental withdrawal symptoms. Withdrawal causes cravings and discomfort, so it can be tough to endure. Because of this, some recovering addicts prefer to detox as inpatients, remaining under the supervision of hospital personnel. If they need help with anxiety or pain, they can easily receive it in a hospital setting. Others, though, choose to detox at home. Outpatient detox works well for those who feel certain that they can stay off stimulants and promise to enroll themselves in a drug treatment program as soon as their detox is complete.

Volunteers sort through donations at San Francisco's Haight Ashbury Clinic. The clinic offers immediate medical care and a recovery program for cocaine and methamphetamine addicts.

Avoiding Cues

Once the drugs are out of the body and the person's physical needs are met, the mental and emotional work can begin: learning to cope with problems without turning to drugs. One recovering addict says that counseling helped him understand that he used coke and meth to camouflage the real emotional issues in his life. Looking back, he now realizes that he felt "insecure [and not] worthy of anything in this world."[62] By taking stimulants, he avoided facing, and dealing with, his problems. Now, by finding and expressing feelings instead of ignoring them, he has learned how to deal with his emotions in a safer way.

In counseling, addicts learn how to manage cravings and to avoid risky cues to prevent a relapse. Cues are stimuli, like friends, places, or drug paraphernalia, that a person associates with the stimulant's effects and that can trigger strong desires for the drugs. In both cocaine and meth addiction, relapse rates are highest when addicts do not avoid their old cues.

Some cues are much harder to avoid than others. Maryaka, a young mother, found that her strongest cues were the people who had been a part of her life when she was using drugs: her friends, her parents, and even her daughter, Krystal. To end her destructive relationship with stimulants, Maryaka had to get away from all of the reminders of her past drug life, including these family members. The hardest one for her to give up was her daughter. Eventually, she let Krystal move in with her father who lives in another state. For Maryaka, letting Krystal go was part of her own recovery. "If I see her, I know I'll relapse. I have to think of myself, and seeing her is one of my triggers to use."[63]

The Matrix

Patients continue their counseling in either an inpatient or outpatient setting. Currently, many clinics are using the Matrix model, a method of outpatient therapy that is backed by research from the Center for Substance Abuse Treatment (CSAT). Over a four- to six-month period, clients take part in treatment for their minds as well as their bodies. They attend at least three group or individual therapy sessions per week where they receive coaching and support.

Straight Talk

Diana is a nineteen-year-old recovered addict. She was addicted to both meth and cocaine in high school. Today, she talks to kids whenever she gets a chance to tell them about her addiction and recovery. The *East Central Minnesota Post Review* covered her story in "Teen Gives Straight Talk on Addiction."

Diana had tried other drugs, but on the night of the junior-senior prom, she says, "I tried meth for the first time. I liked it and I was addicted that first time." Diana says that she stayed high for one whole year. "I surrounded myself with other people who were getting high all the time." When she finally realized that drugs were not making her happy, Diana confessed to her parents that she was an addict. The next day, they enrolled her in a treatment program, but she lasted only two weeks. She went back to school and started using again. In no time, an accidental overdose landed her in the hospital.

Diana moved to an inpatient facility, where she finally made up her mind to stay sober, and she has succeeded. After returning to school, she graduated as valedictorian of her class. Now she is a college student, excited at the prospects of graduating and getting a job and apartment. "My friends have showed me that life is so much more fun without drugs. There are so many other things to do."

In addition, they go to family therapy, take part in relapse prevention treatment, and participate in frequent progress checkups with urine tests to confirm that drugs are no longer being used. The Matrix plan also encourages clients to attend a community-based, self-help program, such as the twelve-step program. Twelve-step groups, found in almost every community, teach that recovery from addiction is an ongoing process that requires continual work. All of this work pays off: After one year, 60 percent of the clients who follow the Matrix plan are still no longer using stimulants.

An anonymous addict who identifies himself as SFJ says that the Matrix-style treatment worked well for him:

I am a methamphetamine addict. It would be more precise to say, "I was an addict." I quit using September 14, 2001. . . . I am now in an intensive outpatient program. I go to therapy every day, individual counseling on a weekly basis, and medical psychiatric counseling every other week. . . . It has been a positive experience.

SFJ encourages others to be patient and give a treatment program time to work. "It takes as long to recover as it did to quit. For example, if you used two years, it takes two years to recover."[64]

Matrix Model

Cognitive process during addiction

Phase	Triggers	Strength of Condition Connection	Responses
Introductory	• Parties • Special occasions	Mild	• Pleasant thoughts about stimulant • No physiological response • Infrequent use
Abuse	• Parties • Friday nights • Friends • Concerts • Alcohol • "Good times" • Sexual situations	Moderate	• Thought of stimulant • Eager anticipation of stimulant use • Mild physiological arousal • Cravings occur as use approaches • Occasional use
Addictional	• Weekends • All friends • Stress • Boredom • Anxiety • After work • Loneliness	Strong	• Continual thoughts of stimulant • Strong physiological arousal • Physiological dependency • Strong cravings • Frequent use
Severe	• Any emotion • Day • Night • Work • Nonwork	Overpowering	• Obsessive thoughts about stimulant • Powerful autonomic response • Powerful physiological dependency • Strong cravings • Automatic use

Extended Care

Addicts who need more structure and guidance can join inpatient programs. The standard inpatient plan is a twenty-eight-day stay in a hospital or residential treatment facility. Each day clients participate in self-help groups and group therapy and practice relaxation techniques. Inpatient programs are designed to be supportive yet confrontational enough to force clients to face their problems and get actively involved in their own treatment.

Long-term residential treatment is good for those who cannot, for social or psychological reasons, return to the community after inpatient treatment. Such programs can help clients make permanent changes in their attitudes about drugs and their lifestyles. Programs generally vary in length from ninety days to one year. In most cases, some of the support staff includes recovering stimulant addicts, people who are uniquely qualified to understand the problems facing their clients.

One type of long-term treatment is the therapeutic community (TC). The TC is a highly structured environment where addicts participate in regularly scheduled group activities that help them reevaluate their lifestyles, attitudes, and values. TCs strongly emphasize the addicts' own responsibility for their choices and behaviors, and they help addicts learn life skills and self-reliance. Many clients are referred to these facilities by the court system.

When clients graduate from TCs, they often move to halfway houses, where they still receive support but have more freedom to come and go as they please. Betty, who started taking cocaine at the age of twelve, says, "I never felt like I fit in. I had a lot of insecurities." After eighteen months in prison on drug charges, she was released to a halfway house. Once she was out of prison, she was terrified that she would revert to her old drug habits. But counselors in the halfway house helped her adjust. Betty found the halfway house to be a warm, secure place where she could recover. "I compare my experience at the House to that of a child who has hurt herself. She goes to her parent to get her boo-boo kissed. She still has the boo-boo, but she feels better."[65]

A Brain on Meth

Even though cocaine and methamphetamine have similar dangers, many doctors believe that meth addiction is more difficult to treat than cocaine addiction. Mounting evidence strongly suggests that the early changes in brain tissue caused by meth may be permanent. If ongoing research proves this to be the case, a shortfall of neurotransmitters in the brains of meth users cannot be reversed, resulting in reduced mental function and loss of motor skills.

Cocaine users recover normal neurotransmitter production after a few weeks of their last use of the drug. Former meth users, however, still experience extremely low levels for months or years. A person with low levels of neurotransmitters feels tired and depressed and has trouble with higher-level reasoning skills like problem solving. As a result, it is hard for them to commit to and stick with a treatment program.

In Search of a Medical Treatment

Armed with this information and much more, the National Institute on Drug Abuse is involved in research on several fronts to find a medical treatment to lessen or reverse the damage caused by stimulant abuse. Some researchers are working on bringing medications to the market that can reverse damage to brain cells. Another group of scientists is working with a medicine that improves the body's ability to make neurotransmitters and help restore normal levels. Elsewhere, scientists are working with antidepressants, chemicals that seem to help addicts deal with the inevitable lows.

In other research, scientists are experimenting with a drug that prevents cocaine from stimulating the brain. In one lab, a cocaine vaccine with the code name TA-CD is under development. Cocaine is a very small molecule, so it can travel through the protective blood-brain barrier that is designed to keep foreign matter away from the brain. It is also too small to be recognized by the body's immune system. However, TA-CD stimulates the immune system to recognize cocaine and then make protective molecules, called antibodies, against it. When antibodies attach to them, cocaine molecules become too large to enter the brain. The hope is that the vaccination will keep cocaine out of a patient's brain and therefore prevent it from producing its characteristic high.

Scientists are also looking at a drug that may help reduce cravings. N-acetyl cysteine, or NAC, can eliminate the rewards associated with cocaine use. So far, NAC has only been tested on rats, but it is now ready for human trials. According to researchers at the Medical University of South Carolina, NAC works by boosting levels of glutamate, a neurotransmitter, in the brain. Glutamate levels rapidly increase when cocaine is ingested but decrease significantly in the brains of regular cocaine users. Dr. David Baker found that "treatment with n-acetyl cysteine not only restores glutamate to normal levels but also prevents glutamate levels from sharply increasing following subsequent injections."[66]

Alternatives to Jail Time

In the 1980s, judges were held to strict sentencing guidelines for drug offenses. But when the same offenders kept appearing in court over and over again, the legal system decided that time in jail was not solving the problem. As a result, a new program called Family Dependency Drug Court was implemented.

Twenty-one-year-old Zigmond Gryzbowski Jr. was arrested in August 2001 due to meth use. Ten years ago, a judge would have sent the young man straight to prison. But because of changes in the sentencing of drug addicts in Kitsap County, Washington, Gryzbowski was able to check into a treatment center and participate in Family Dependency Drug Court.

This program reflects a shift in philosophy to one that focuses more on treating the cause of stimulant addiction rather than punishing users. The family dependency court is being piloted in several Washington counties. The addicts and their families meet in court weekly. All have been through drug treatment programs and are involved in ongoing work with drug counselors to fight addiction. "[The family dependency court] creates a web of support so if they start to slip, we can catch them as quick as they fall," coordinator Cherie West tells Angela Smith with *SunLink.com*.

The program is young, but it seems to be working for Gryzbowski and many others. According to West, "There are some people who blow it, . . . but there are a lot of successes."

There Is Good News

To date, the best treatment results are seen when an addict takes advantage of an array of techniques, such as medication, counseling, and behavioral therapy. Many medical professionals liken the healing of an addicted brain to the recovery of a broken leg: The injured body part needs medical support, safety, and enough time to successfully complete the healing process.

Addicts who join inpatient programs stay in residential treatment facilities for a month or more where they receive structure, guidance, and constant support.

Mark Miller knows that recovery is a lifetime commitment. Mark, who started using meth in his late twenties, first entered treatment in 1999 at the age of thirty-five, suffered a relapse, and then returned in 2000. Journalist Jon Bonné reports that even though it has been a struggle, Mark is doing well and keeping busy. He is

> working at Gold's Gym and exercising every day. He takes antidepressant medication, attends church on Sunday, and goes to recovery group meetings almost daily. . . . [Mark] acknowledges that he could easily feel sorry for himself, but he says part of the healing process has been learning to cope with how his life turned out. [He says,] "I don't have to be a crybaby about it."[67]

Since stimulant addicts are a diverse group, no two patients experience the same results or heal on the same schedule. Ultimately, the work of recovery is done by the addicts themselves. They are the ones who must make difficult decisions and stick with them. Their reward is an opportunity to return to life as they knew it before stimulant addiction.

Chapter 5

Challenges of Stamping Out Stimulants

Illegal stimulants are big business all over the world. Across the United States, where illegal drugs are in great demand, sales of cocaine and methamphetamine are brisk. For thirty years, drug enforcement agencies in the United States have tirelessly attacked the illegal stimulant business on multiple fronts. Sources and shipments of stimulants have been destroyed, leaders of drug organizations have been arrested, and stimulant users have been sent to prison, treatment centers, or both. Nevertheless, Americans continue to have access to and use these dangerous drugs.

How can authorities most effectively stop the endless flow of illegal stimulants into the U.S. market? They direct most of their efforts at investigating the origins of the two most dangerous illegal stimulants marketed on American soil, cocaine and methamphetamine, and then they attack these drugs at their sources. For cocaine, which is grown in foreign countries, this means halting shipments before they arrive in the United States. For meth, authorities locate and destroy the laboratories where it is made.

From Leaf to Lab

Most of the cocaine sold in the United States has its roots in the hilly countrysides of Colombia and Peru. Growers pick their crops of coca leaves every three or four days and then carry the harvest to a nearby lab. There, the first step required to purify cocaine from coca leaves takes place: The leaves are converted to cocaine paste. With every step of cocaine processing, profits skyrocket. It takes about 250 pounds of coca leaves, several crops that net the farmer only $150, to make a pound of cocaine paste. Each pound of paste is then sold to a dealer in a nearby city for about $1,500. Dealers finish processing the paste into consumable cocaine, which they sell to customers in the United States for about $15,000. The price hike between paste in South America and product in the United States reflects the risks involved in smuggling cocaine into the country.

Colombian farmworkers gather coca leaves. Most of the cocaine sold in the United States comes from Colombia.

Worldwide production, sales, and distribution of cocaine are controlled by organized criminal groups based in Colombia. The heads of these groups are dubbed "drug lords." According to cocaine historian Mike Gray, Colombia's geography is ideal for cocaine trafficking:

> The country's position at the top of the continent made it the natural jumping-off place for United States–bound traffic, and its access to ports on both the Pacific and Caribbean combined with native hustle [eagerness to work hard] to create a hot-house environment for smugglers.[68]

Drug lords work closely with organized crime in Mexico and the Dominican Republic. Together, the multinational groups form private armies that specialize in transporting cocaine across land, air, and sea. One of their favorite delivery routes uses entry points along the border between the United States and Mexico.

Sneaking In

Much of the two-thousand-mile southern U.S. border is uninhabited, wide-open space. However, in places where there are people, towns, and roads, border patrol agents regulate travel, trying to slow the stream of drugs into the United States. Customs inspector Tom Isbell has been guarding the border for twenty-six years. Isbell says that he and his men cannot stop and search every vehicle that is lined up to pass through the border checkpoints. Instead, they watch the vehicles and try to spot drivers who look tense, vigilant, or scared. Isbell has an excellent record for picking out cars and vans carrying drugs. "It's an instinct," he shrugs. Isbell and his fellow workers seize large quantities—hundreds of pounds—of drugs. But compared to the amount of drugs that make it across the border, their seizures are small. According to Isbell, "We intercept maybe five percent."[69]

At sea, one of the most popular cocaine delivery paths is from Colombia to the western coast of Mexico or the Yucatán peninsula. Workers load large boxes filled with illicit cargo onto fishing boats at Colombian ports and unload the boats in Mexico. There, the big shipping crates of cocaine are divided into smaller parcels that can be inconspicuously carried over the U.S. border. A less hectic marine route is through the Caribbean. Drug lords use Puerto Rico, the Dominican Republic, and Haiti as cocaine drops. Much of the cocaine traveling through these islands is destined for the eastern United States.

Beres Spence, the chief of the narcotics division of Haiti's police force, has his hands full: "Where we used to see maybe one boatload of cocaine a week, we're now seeing three to four boatloads of cocaine, each weighing 800 to 1,800 pounds." Compounding matters, the Haitian shoreline is extensive, and his law enforcement teams are scattered thin in their efforts to secure it. Despite his efforts, many smugglers enter undetected. As Spence explains, "Traffickers can access every inch of our shoreline, but it would be impossible for us to cover every inch."[70]

In her job as a reporter for ABC News, Deborah Amos has witnessed the kind of problems Spence has to deal with. She says, "The cocaine flow in the Caribbean has increased approximately 60 percent [from 1999 to 2002], and the flow in Haiti has increased about 50 percent." What makes the problem difficult to deal with is that "the methods for smuggling drugs are both impressive and elaborate." For example, Amos recalled an incident in which "customs agents hauled five freighters out of the water after an informant told them where to search. They found $25 million worth of cocaine stashed in secret compartments four floors below deck, covered by fuel oil and thick sludge. . . . These ships often go unnoticed in the busy port of Miami."[71]

Jamaica is another convenient shipping hub. Located halfway between South America and the United States, Jamaica sees cocaine that may be en route to Europe, Canada, or the United States. Shipments destined for the United States are loaded on fast boats that travel close to the Florida shore. From there the shipments are transferred onto pleasure boats or fishing boats for distribution along the coast.

All of this illegal activity has substantially increased the workload of the U.S. Coast Guard. According to the Office of National

*Police arrest drug traffickers in Bogotá, Colombia. The traffickers'
cocaine, packaged in the brick-sized parcels, was destined for the United
States.*

Drug Control Policy, the Coast Guard has geared up to meet the
challenge by

> acquiring new equipment, developing new capabilities, and changing use-
> of-force policies. [For example,] initial deployments of specially config-
> ured helicopters and pursuit boats utilizing a new policy of warning shots
> and disabling fire [gunfire meant to slow boats that are evading the Coast
> Guard] was highly successful, resulting in the seizure of 3,014 pounds of
> cocaine . . . in a two month period [in 1999].[72]

Tactics to Crush Coca

The federal government knows that, unfortunately, it cannot stop all
cocaine from entering the United States. So, it has adopted another
strategy, one that focuses on eliminating the source of the problem,
the coca plants themselves. Several programs have been devised to
destroy coca plants, such as spraying the plants with herbicide or cut-
ting them down. Efforts to teach farmers how to raise legal crops in
their place have been tried in the past and are still under way today.
So far, these plant-elimination tactics seem to help temporarily, but
most farmers eventually return to the lucrative coca business.

In the past, the United States has received little support from political leaders in South America in its efforts to slow the production of coca. However, that situation has changed recently. Colombia's current president, Alvaro Uribe, is interested in working with the United States to get rid of coca in his country. He has launched an assault on coca crops that is intended to cripple the industry. According to Amos, Uribe promises to make "Colombia drug-free by the end of his term in 2006."[73] U.S. officials believe that Uribe's position will eventually reduce the supply of cocaine.

Speed on the Market

Unlike cocaine, methamphetamine is usually manufactured in the United States. After amphetamines were first introduced in the 1920s, enterprising chemists in California figured out how to make the drugs for themselves. With a little research and experimentation, home-based chemists also came up with the recipe for the more potent form, methamphetamine. Illegal labs for manufacturing speed sprang up almost overnight on the West Coast.

These labs developed in many shapes and sizes. Dr. Roger Smith's 1969 report on the "Speed Marketplace" explains the diversity of these early labs:

> A speed laboratory may range from a well organized, highly efficient operation, capable of producing five to twenty five pounds [from about 225,000 to about 1,125,000 ten-milligram doses] of speed per week consistently, to a kitchen or bathroom in a small apartment, producing less than an ounce per week, to a college chemistry laboratory where a student produces speed only occasionally, when he needs money or feels that the chances of detection are slight.[74]

Criminal organizations based in California controlled the recipes, manufacture, sales, and distribution of meth. For twenty years, meth sales remained concentrated in California and a few nearby states, so law enforcement initially assessed meth as a local problem. However, by the early 1990s, gangs had decided to capitalize on the popular West Coast drug and expand their market. With a made-for-order system in place, meth production grew into a national moneymaking enterprise.

Success attracts attention, and it was not long before gangs in Mexico established their own superlabs south of the border. Meth was easily smuggled into the United States along with cocaine; then both drugs were dispersed through the cocaine distribution networks. Once the professional drug traffickers got into the business, meth's popularity quickly spread across the country.

Mom and Pop Take Chemistry

With the advent of the Internet, gangs and Mexican drug cartels lost their exclusive ownership of meth recipes. Directions for whipping up a batch of meth became easy to come by. As a result, tiny meth labs began to appear across the United States. Today these small labs, along with the major California and Mexican manufacturers, are the primary providers of meth.

Although Mexican and Californian labs crank out meth in large quantities of twenty pounds or more per cook, many users prefer to buy from small local labs. Amateur chemists set up what some law enforcement officers call "Mom and Pop" labs in homes, storage facilities, motels, and open fields. Unless an informant tips off police officers, these labs are very difficult for them to find. Most do not operate full-time, gearing up to cook meth only when a new batch is needed. Many are mobile labs whisked from one place to another in the backs of vans and trunks of cars. One police officer on routine patrol found a man making meth in his car in the parking lot of a high school.

Lab Busts

Once they are found, busting at-home meth labs is serious and dangerous work. Police have to deal with the booby traps that paranoid meth cooks use to protect themselves from intruders. It is not unusual to find attack dogs tied to front and back doors and guns and ammunition hidden around the lab. All of these elements create a risky situation.

Journalist Jon Bonné joined the Pierce County sheriff's meth lab team on a busy workday. Bonné describes the tense prepara-

A Meth Cook's Story

The life of an illegal drug manufacturer is put in sharp perspective in "A Meth Cook Speaks from Prison." Posted on the Web site the New Lycaeum, this article, written by a former meth cook who is now in jail, gives some sage advice for those who think that stirring up a batch of meth is no big deal.

Some people out there seem to think that the Federal Prison is a "cake-walk" but it's not. . . . Imagine your bathroom with a bunk bed in place of the bathtub, and a desk and two lockers jammed in there. That's my room. I share that with a roommate. . . . Life here is very monotonous. Nothing ever changes except the date and the faces. Someone tells you when to eat, sleep, stand, work. . . . If you don't play the game by their rules, they can make this a very unpleasant experience. Believe me, none of you want to come here. . . . I live in a nightmare and I've been here so long that I've almost forgotten what physical human contact feels like. I don't remember what it's like to get in my car and go to the store. Okay, maybe I did deserve to come here. I was actually manufacturing methamphetamine on a large scale for personal greed and amusement. I'm not disputing that fact. I'm just writing in hopes that my post will open the eyes of some of you. . . . You see . . . I have nothing to lose.

tions for a meth lab bust: "In the town's small courtroom, 20 officers are briefed. . . . Team members review aerial photos and share details of how the bust will unfold. . . . The officers don tactical assault gear—body armor, headsets and helmets—and prepare to head out." At the bust site, tensions remain high. Bonné continues:

A convoy of about a dozen vehicles winds its way across town to the bust site. Deputies leap out and shout, "Police! Search warrant!" as they bust into the backyard shack where the suspect lives. . . . The suspect appears taken by surprise and is quickly cuffed.

The deputies, along with local officers and DEA [Drug Enforcement Administration] agents, fan out across the property, which is covered with overgrowth and littered with the hulks of rusting trucks and campers. They move through the high brush in a single file, alert for possible snipers or hidden evidence. The sheriff's raid command center, a modified recreational vehicle with "Pierce County Clandestine Lab Team" painted on the side, pulls into the driveway to process whatever substances the deputies find.[75]

From a law enforcement point of view, these small labs may be more troublesome than large factories like those in Mexico and California because they are difficult to locate. The DEA explains that the proliferation of meth labs has spread the drug across the United States. In Alabama, for example, the problem is growing rapidly. "We trip over meth labs here,"[76] says Chuck Phillips, chief investigator of the Jackson County Sheriff's Department. In neighboring Tennessee, there were two meth lab busts in the entire state in 1996. In 2002 there were more than four hundred. The same is true nationwide. The DEA reports an alarming upsurge in labs and lab busts. In 1994 the DEA seized 263 meth labs. By the year

Small, portable meth labs like this one enable methamphetamine cooks to make the drug anywhere and to avoid police detection.

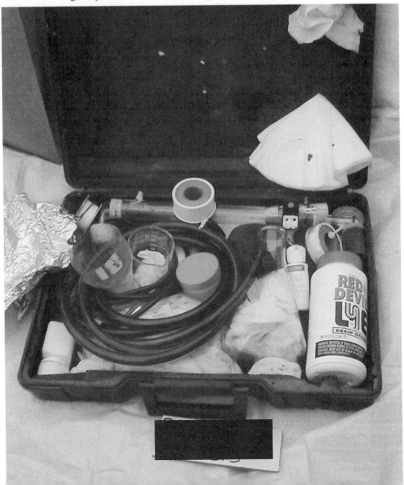

A Day in the Coca Fields

With the help of Colombian president Alvaro Uribe, the U.S. government has enacted a plan to destroy Colombia's coca crops. Steve Nettleton, a correspondent for CNN, visited Colombia to speak to the workers who may soon be affected by this plan. There he met one young family man who is trying to make a living by picking coca leaves.

His callused hands smeared with lime-green resin, Francisco slides his fingers along the stems of coca plants, shearing off the leaves in one fluid motion. He collects the severed leaves on a small tarp and moves to bare the next shrub of its foliage.

Francisco, who offered only his first name, is a *raspachín*, or "scraper"—the name Colombians give to coca pickers for the rough manner with which they harvest their crop. He is paid by farm owners to process the coca into a milky-white paste, called coca base, which is sold to traffickers to be crystallized into cocaine.

His salary is better than most farm laborers. At 300,000 pesos a month (U.S.$136), he earns enough for himself, though not enough for his entire family. But close exposure to the chemicals and gasoline used to make coca base makes you age faster, he said. And the job comes with a curse.

"The money in this work is evil money," he said. "You get corrupted making money with this, because of what you do with it. A lot of people who work with me have become addicted [to drinking]. They spend all their money on [alcohol]."

Yet, for all the hardships, being a *raspachín* is the best Francisco can do in these southern jungles of Colombia. He would rather work as a cattle rancher, but he has no land and no money to begin such an enterprise.

For Francisco, like many poor Colombians, life offers few choices. Efforts by the Colombian government to end the production of coca will take away the only job Francisco can get. But Francisco will go on. "This is going to end; it's not going on forever," he said. "[When it does end] I'll do whatever life gives me."

2000, there were 1,815 labs seized, a 590 percent increase. That same year, state and local agencies found another 4,600 labs.

Hooked on Cooking

With the proliferation of meth labs, and of cooks who take their job seriously, a strange "meth chef" culture has arisen. "A lot of people here [love] the cooking aspect—it's almost a social phenomenon among people who do that," says Charles Rhodes, a district attorney in Jackson County, Tennessee. "You find two or three or four people getting together in a house or trailer, they cook some up then move to another house and cook some more. It's like a potluck."[77]

Barry Kennamer, a former firefighter and family man who is now in prison, loved cooking. For Barry, making meth was almost as exciting as taking it, and he spent hours perfecting his recipe: "You see somebody cook it one time, and it sweeps you off your feet. You take these chemicals, get a big reaction, and that acid smell. . . . Man, I don't know what it is about cooking, but it can flat take you away."[78]

What most cooks rarely acknowledge, however, is how dangerous the job is. Of the thirty-two different chemicals that can be used, more than one-third of them are extremely dangerous. Undiluted hydriodic acid, for example, is highly caustic. Red phosphorous, a flammable compound, can be converted to phosphine gas, one of the deadly nerve gases used in World War I. Red phosphorous is also the cause of many of the fires in meth labs. One-quarter of all meth labs catch fire before being discovered.

One method of making meth is favored by many because it is fast, cheap, and requires very little equipment. It involves toxic ingredients like lithium, a component of batteries, and anhydrous ammonia, an ingredient in fertilizer. Some of the other dangerous chemicals that can be used in meth production include iodine, ether, chloroform, drain cleaner, lighter fluid, and propane.

Hazards to Children of Meth Chefs

Because it uses such dangerous chemicals, the production of meth not only takes a toll on the bodies of the meth cooks but impacts a much wider circle of people, such as their children, law enforcement officers, and neighbors. Meth is even bad for the environment.

Children are found during more than half of meth lab busts. The kids of meth cookers live in an environment of toxic chemicals and potentially explosive reactions. Their lungs are exposed to caustic fumes that cause bronchitis and lung infections. Many exist in filthy conditions, often without food, for days on end while their parents are bingeing. It is not unusual for parents to lock their children in a room while they are cooking and using and then forget to let them out. Children who are found during a meth bust are taken into protective custody.

In an interview with journalist Caitlin Rother, one pediatrician relates some of the horrors she has witnessed firsthand. Dr. Wendy Wright, who works with Children's Hospital and the Polinsky Children's Center in San Diego, sees too many kids in dangerous homes. In one dirty shack, she found meth syringes on the floor,

Drug enforcement agents examine chemicals removed from a home after local firefighters responded to a house fire. A meth lab operating in the home started the fire.

bottles of toxic chemicals stored in the refrigerator next to identi-
cal containers of soda, and an unsupervised two-year-old roaming
the premises. "Not only are children in physical danger," Wright
warns, "they are learning how to use meth themselves."[79]

To make her point, Wright showed a video of five-year-old
Sophia, who described how her parents use meth. "They get a
piece of foil. They make a little roll," the child said. "They get a
lighter and then they light it up. . . . They save it until they do it
again, and they always do it again." When the interviewer asked
Sophia to use crayons to show how many times her parents
smoked the drug again, she piled all of the crayons in a big stack
and looked around for more. "I need more crayons,"[80] she said.

In addition, Wright explained that young children can even tell
her how to manufacture meth. Sadly, many children learn these
skills from family. "If your dad cooks meth in the house, that's
what you're going to learn to do,"[81] says Lieutenant Mel Williams
of the Sioux City, Iowa, police force. Children as young as eight
years old have been found working in meth labs.

Other Dangers Posed by Cooking
Just being the neighbor of a meth cook can have negative consequences. In apartment buildings, toxic meth fumes can be carried
through an entire building along central heat and air conditioning
ducts. Neighbors living in houses next to meth cooks encounter
irritating fumes and odors. And when meth cooks move, they
rarely clean up the residue from their dangerous chemicals, thus
exposing the next renters or home buyers to a variety of toxins.
Just lingering where there are fumes can make a person sick.

Cooks have no regard for the environment and dump their
waste chemicals wherever convenient. The amount of waste produced by labs is enormous. For every pound of final product, five
or six pounds of chemical waste are generated. Hazardous ingredients get poured down drains, where they flow directly into
plants that treat wastewater for return to streams or watersheds.
In rural areas, cooks often empty hazardous materials right onto
the ground, where they can seep into the groundwater. The cost

of cleanup at a meth site can be thousands of dollars and put police who discover and dismantle these labs at risk.

The Work Continues

To battle cocaine and meth use, several states have set aside funds for dealing with abuse of stimulants, allocating money for seizing drugs, arresting sellers, treating addicts, and educating the public. In the Midwest, the DEA has created the High Intensity Drug Trafficking Area program. Its job is to coordinate the efforts of law enforcement to combat methamphetamine activity in North and South Dakota, Iowa, Kansas, Missouri, and Nebraska. By pulling together local agencies in those areas, the program makes it difficult for clandestine labs to pull up roots and move to a neighboring state.

Every state law enforcement agency receives federal backup and support in the war against stimulants. To focus attention on the "meth epidemic," Congress instituted the Methamphetamine Interagency Task Force in 1998. It has created a multifaceted approach to the problem that includes the establishment of task forces on the local level, the promotion of education to foster prevention, and improvement in treatment. The task force also provides money, expertise, and technical assistance to communities.

Plans are under development to create an early warning system, an identification of trends in a geographical area that indicate increases in stimulant abuse. Once an area has been identified as high risk, resources can be allocated to it. Plans are also moving forward to create a community resource guide, a set of materials about illegal stimulants that local citizens can use to help them teach the dangers of stimulant use and learn about treatment programs and law enforcement resources. By attacking the problem on all fronts, the United States is learning the most effective methods in stamping out stimulant use.

Notes

Chapter 1: A Brief History of Stimulants

1. Andrew Weil and Winifred Rosen, *From Chocolate to Morphine*. New York: Houghton Mifflin, 1993, pp. 38–39.
2. Cynthia Kuhn, Scott Swartzwelder, and Wilkie Wilson, *Buzzed*. New York: W.W. Norton, 1998, p. 57.
3. Quoted in Edward M. Brecher, "Caffeine," *The Consumers Union Report on Licit and Illicit Drugs*, Schaffer Library, 1972. www. druglibrary.org/schaffer.
4. Robert Shmerling, "Are There Grounds for Concern?" *Harvard Commentary Health News*, May 25, 2001. www. intelihealth.com.
5. Quoted in Gene Borio, "Tobacco Timeline," *Tobacco.org*, 2001. www.tobacco.org.
6. Quoted in Borio, "Tobacco Timeline."
7. Quoted in Cabell Smith, "Medical Uses for Nicotine," *Dukemed News*, August 10, 2001. www.dukemednews. duke.edu.
8. Quoted in Glen Hanson, Peter Venturelli, and Annette Fleckenstein, *Drugs and Society*. Boston: Jones & Bartlett, 2002, p. 263.
9. Brecher, "Cocaine."
10. Brecher, "Cocaine."
11. Quoted in *Good Drug Guide*, "Crack Cocaine: A Once-in-a-Lifetime Experience?" n.d. http://cocaine.org.
12. Quoted in *Good Drug Guide*, "Vintage Wine."
13. Neil Swan, "Brain Scan Opens Window to View Cocaine's Effects on the Brain," *NIDA Notes*, July 1998. www.drugabuse.gov.

Chapter 2: Stimulant Abuse

14. Edward Huntington Williams, "Negro Cocaine Fiends, New Southern Menace," in Brecher, *The Consumers Union Report on Licit and Illicit Drugs*.

15. Harold E. Doweiko, *Concepts of Chemical Dependency*. London: Brook/Cole Thomson Learning, 2002, p. 124.
16. Quoted in Andrew Scutro, "The Meth Behind the Madness," *Idaho Mountain Express*, April 22, 1998. www.mtexpress.com.
17. Quoted in Scutro, "The Meth Behind the Madness."
18. Quoted in Ken Olsen, "A Health Peril for All of Us," *MSNBC News*, 1999. www.msnbc.com.
19. Quoted in "Channeling the Energy," Amphetamine Experiences, *Interdope*, n.d. www.interdope.com.
20. Cynric, "Jacked: Thirty Hours and Beyond," *Erowid Experience Vaults*, June 23, 2000. www.erowid.org/experiences.
21. Nash, "Excuse Me . . . but May I Have Some More?" *Erowid Experience Vaults*, July 2002. www.erowid.org/experiences.
22. Matt Schofield, "Addict, Area Take Steps to Handle Problem," *Kansas City Star*, November 12, 1998. www.kcstar.com.
23. Quoted in Conrad Evarts, "Twelve Hours with a Meth Addict," *Pulp Syndicate*, 2003. www.pulpsyndicate.com.
24. Doweiko, *Concepts of Chemical Dependency*, p. 143.
25. Carlos A. Perez, "My Kind of Life: Crystal Death—Amphetamine," *Positively Aware*, July/August 2003. www.thebody.com.
26. Quoted in NBC4.TV News, "Extreme Speed," May 3, 2003. www.nbc4.tv.
27. Quoted in NBC4.TV News, "Extreme Speed."
28. Quoted in NBC4.TV News, "Extreme Speed."
29. Steven, "The Party's Over," *Tweaker.org*, n.d. www.tweaker.org/stories.
30. Schofield, "Addict, Area Take Steps to Handle Problem."
31. Quoted in NBC4.TV News, "Extreme Speed."

Chapter 3: Dangers of Stimulant Addiction

32. Quoted in Hanson, Venturelli, and Fleckenstein, *Drugs and Society*, p. 87.
33. Paul M. Gahlinger, *Illegal Drugs*. Las Vegas: Sagebrush Press, 2001, p. 98.
34. Quoted in Jesse Sowa, "Green Schools," *Corvallis [OR] Gazette Times*, March 1, 2003. www.gazettetimes.com.

35. Nicole Hansen, "Real Drugs, False Friends: The Nicole Hansen Story," *DrugFreeAZ.com*, n.d. www.drugfreeaz.com.
36. Lyn, "I Am in Recovery Now, but This Was My Life as an Addict," *Recovery Site*, n.d. http://lynnfromct.freeyellow.com/addiction.html.
37. Kuhn, Swartzwelder, and Wilson, *Buzzed*, p. 243.
38. Hanson, Venturelli, and Fleckenstein, *Drugs and Society*, p. 31.
39. David Satcher, "A Call for Action: Surgeon General's Report, Reducing Tobacco Use," April 3, 2003. www.cdc.gov.
40. Sky, "My Story," *Meth Madness*, 2002. www.meth madness.com.
41. Olsen, "A Health Peril for All of Us."
42. Quoted in Olsen, "A Health Peril for All of Us."
43. T.M., "The Shadow People," *CrystalRecovery.com*, n.d. www.crystalrecovery.com.
44. Quoted in Brad Zellar, "Embedded in Austin," *City Pages* [Minneapolis, MN], May 14, 2003. www.citypages.com.
45. Quoted in Pamela Hill, "When High Wears Off, Paranoia, Health Woes Lurk," *Arkansas Democrat-Gazette*, June 7, 1999. www.ardemgaz.com.
46. Quoted in *Robert Downey Jr., New Beginnings* "An Addict's True Story," n.d. www.geocities.com.
47. Quoted in Yale University, "Cocaine Use Decreases Ability to Respond to Stimulation, Yale Researchers Find," February 23, 2001. www.yale.edu/opa.
48. Quoted in Zellar, "Embedded in Austin."
49. Quoted in "Confessions of a White Collar Cocaine Addict: From Ruin to Renewal," n.d. http://home.wi.rr.com.
50. Quoted in Medical Online, "Drugs and Drug Abuse: Cocaine," n.d. www.medicalonline.com.au.
51. Olsen, "A Health Peril for All of Us."
52. Olsen, "A Health Peril for All of Us."
53. Quoted in Olsen, "A Health Peril for All of Us."
54. Jon Bonné, "Meth's Deadly Buzz," *MSNBC News*, 2003. www.msnbc.com.

Chapter 4: Treatment for Stimulant Addiction

55. Quoted in Hanson, Venturelli, and Fleckenstein, *Drugs and Society*, p. 319.

56. Dinah, "Dinah's Story," *Quit Smoking*, n.d. www.quit-smoking.net/stories.
57. American Lung Association, "New Survey Shows Consumer Confusion, Loss of Ritual Limit Stop-Smoking Success," September 9, 1998. www.lungusa.org.
58. Quoted in New York State Department of Health "Thinking About Stopping Smoking?" n.d. www.health.state.ny.us.
59. K.R., "Just Wanted to Have Fun," *CrystalRecovery.com*, n.d. www.crystalrecovery.com.
60. Koch Crime Institute, "Methamphetamine Frequently Asked Questions," n.d. www.kci.org.
61. Quoted in Jon Bonné, "Hooked in the Haight," *MSNBC News*, 2003. www.msnbc.com.
62. Quoted in Bonné, "Hooked in the Haight."
63. Quoted in Art Merrill, "Methamphetamine White Lies," *Prescott Valley Tribune*, n.d. www.prescottaz.com.
64. Quoted in Mike Mosedale, "Meth Myths, Meth Realities," *City Pages* [Minneapolis, MN], May 14, 2003. www.citypages.com/databank.
65. Quoted in "Success Stories," *Welcome to Mrs. Wilson's*, n.d. www.mrswilsons.org.
66. Quoted in BBC News, "Drug Could Help Cocaine Addicts," December 9, 2002. http://news.bbc.co.uk.
67. Bonné, "Hooked in the Haight."

Chapter 5: Challenges of Stamping Out Stimulants

68. Mike Gray, *Drug Crazy*, New York: Random House, 1998, p. 118.
69. Quoted in Gray, *Drug Crazy*, p. 146.
70. Quoted in Matthew J. Rosenberg, "Jamaica Struggles to Contain Boom—Coke Smuggling," *Cannabis News*, February 9, 2000. www.cannabisnews.com.
71. Deborah Amos, "New Battlefield," *ABCNews.com*, May 16, 2002. http://abcnews.go.com.
72. Office of National Drug Control Policy, "The National Drug Control Strategy 2000 Annual Report," n.d. www.ncjrs.org.
73. Amos, "New Battlefield."
74. Quoted in Edward M. Brecher, "Amphetamines."
75. Jon Bonné, "Lab-Busting in the Northwest," *MSNBC News*, 2003. www.msnbc.com.

76. Quoted in Drew Jubera, "Moonshine Country Overrun by Meth," *Atlanta Journal and Constitution.* February 9, 2003, p. A1.
77. Quoted in Jubera, "Moonshine Country Overrun by Meth," p. A7.
78. Quoted in Jubera, "Moonshine Country Overrun by Meth," p. A7.
79. Quoted in Caitlin Rother, "Doctor Studies Meth's Impacts on Children," *San Diego Union-Tribune*, February 10, 2003. www.lindesmith.org.
80. Quoted in Rother, "Doctor Studies Meth's Impacts on Children."
81. Quoted in Bonné, "Meth's Deadly Buzz."

Organizations to Contact

Drug Enforcement Administration (DEA)
2401 Jefferson Davis Hwy.
Alexandria, VA 22301
(202) 307-8846
www.usdoj.gov/dea

Maintained by the Department of Justice, the DEA keeps current information on trends in stimulant abuse.

Narcotics Anonymous, World Service
PO Box 9999
Van Nuys, CA 91409
(818) 773-9999
www.na.org/index.htm

Narcotics Anonymous provides successful treatment for drug abuse. Its Web site includes information on local chapters, drug chemistry, and success stories.

National Clearinghouse for Alcohol and Drug Information (NCADI)
11426-28 Rockville Pike, Suite 200
Rockville, MD 20852
(800) 729-6686
www.health.org

NCADI is a resource for obtaining up-to-date information on all types of drugs.

National Families in Action
2957 Clairmont Road
Atlanta, GA 30329
(404) 248-9676
www.nationalfamilies.org

This organization provides information about drugs and how they affect the body, and supplies answers to questions about drugs.

National Institute on Drug Abuse (NIDA)
6001 Executive Blvd., Room 5213
Bethesda, MD 20892-9651
(301) 443-6245
www.drugabuse.gov

NIDA provides information on research into drug abuse, its causes, and its treatments.

For Further Reading

Books

David L. Bender and Bruno Leone, eds., *Chemical Dependency* San Diego, CA: Greenhaven Press, 1997. A collection of articles with opposing points of view on drug use and treatment of drug addiction.

Carol Falkowski, *Dangerous Drugs*. Center City, MN: Hazelden, 2000. Falkowski provides an overview of the way drugs are abused and the extent of their use, as well as explanations on their effects on the body, methods of treatment for drug abuse, and suggestions for prevention.

Paul M. Gahlinger, *Illegal Drugs*. Las Vegas: Sagebrush Press, 2001. A comprehensive review of illegal drugs, drug policy, addiction, and treatment.

Go Ask Alice: A Real Diary. New York: Simon and Schuster, 1971. A gritty, true story of one teen's journey into the world of drug abuse.

Joseph Sora, ed., *Substance Abuse*. New York: H.W. Wilson, 1997. Reprints from books, articles, and addresses on trends in drug use in the United States.

Websites

American Lung Association (www.lungusa.org). Explains the dangers of tobacco and provides suggestions for those who want to stop smoking.

Centers for Disease Control and Prevention (www.cdc.gov). The nation's leading health and safety center provides information to help people make intelligent decisions about health issues.

Fact Monster (www.factmonster.com). Offers links to information on all aspects of stimulant use.

How Stuff Works (www.howstuffworks.com). A great resource for gathering easy-to-read, straightforward information on all types of drugs.

In the Know Zone (www.intheknowzone.com). Provides both historical and current information about the use of stimulants.

Office of National Drug Control Policy (www.whitehouse drugpolicy.gov). The ONDCP establishes policies, priorities, and objectives for the nation's drug control program.

Sara's Quest (www.sarasquest.org). Sara Bellum is a girl on a quest to find out how drugs affect the brain.

The Why Files (http://whyfiles.org). A resource for science news items, including articles on nicotine.

Works Consulted

Books

Harold E. Doweiko, *Concepts of Chemical Dependency*. London: Brook/Cole Thomson Learning, 2002. Explains how drugs cause addiction and what steps can be taken to treat it.

Mike Gray, *Drug Crazy*. New York: Random House, 1998. A history of opium and cocaine use in the United States.

Glen Hanson, Peter Venturelli, and Annette Fleckenstein, *Drugs and Society*. Boston: Jones & Bartlett, 2002. An excellent textbook on drugs of abuse that includes scientific and social perspectives.

Elizabeth Connell Henderson, *Understanding Addiction*. Jackson: University Press of Mississippi, 2000. Designed for the friends and families of addicts, this book explains all aspects of addiction in nonmedical terms.

Jill Jones, *Hep Cats, Narcs, and Pipe Dreams*. New York: Scribner, 1996. Through a collection of essays, Jones describes the history of cocaine use and abuse in the United States.

Cynthia Kuhn, Scott Swartzwelder, and Wilkie Wilson, *Buzzed*. New York: W.W. Norton, 1998. An excellent resource on illicit drugs.

Solomon Snyder, *Drugs and the Brain*. New York: Scientific American Books, 1986. Synder was one of the first scientists to discover how the brain works by studying the impact of different chemicals on brain function. His writings are the definitive works on drugs and the nervous system.

Andrew Weil and Winifred Rosen, *From Chocolate to Morphine.* New York: Houghton Mifflin, 1993. A very readable book that discusses several types of recreational drugs.

Periodicals

Dennis Conrad, "Illinois' Total Bid, Cigarette Ban Has Teens Primarily in Mind," *Jefferson City News Tribune*, December 12, 2002.

Drew Jubera, "Moonshine Country Overrun by Meth," *Atlanta Journal and Constitution*, February 9, 2003.

Greg Miller, "Use of Amphetamines by Pilots in the Military Called into Question," *Los Angeles Times*, January 5, 2003.

Kelly Morris, "Seeking Ways to Crack Cocaine Addiction," *Lancet Publishing Group*, October 17, 1998.

Susan Pennell, *Meth Matters: Report on Methamphetamine.* Washington, DC: U.S. Department of Justice, Office of Justice Programs, April 1999.

Internet Sources

Action for Drug Awareness, "Amphetamines," n.d. www.drugs awareness.co.uk.

American Lung Association, "New Survey Shows Consumer Confusion, Loss of Ritual Limit Stop-Smoking Success," September 9, 1998. www.lungusa.org.

Deborah Amos, "New Battlefield." *ABCNews.com*, May 16, 2002. http://abcnews.go.com.

Robert Bazell, "Flavored Tobacco Has Bitter Effect," *MSNBC News*, December 16, 2002. www.msnbc.com.

BBC News, "Drug Could Help Cocaine Addicts," December 9, 2002. http://news.bbc.co.uk.

———, "Scientists Cast Doubt on Caffeine Addiction," March 22, 1999. http://news.bbc.co.uk.

Kevin Blackistone, "NFL Drug Ban Does Make Sense," *Texas Cable News*, November 23, 2002. www.txcn.com.

Jon Bonné, "Hooked in the Haight," *MSNBC News*, 2003. www.msnbc.com.

———, "Lab-Busting in the Northwest," *MSNBC News*, 2003. www.msnbc.com.

———, "Meth's Deadly Buzz," *MSNBC News*, 2003. www.msnbc.com.

———, "Scourge of the Heartland," *MSNBC News*, 2003. www.msnbc.com.

Gene Borio, "Tobacco Timeline," *Tobacco.org*, 2001. www. tobacco.org.

Shana Bowman, "Caffeine Is Not Diagnosed as an Addiction," *Carolina Reporter*, n.d. http://carolinareporter.sc.edu.

Edward M. Brecher, *The Consumers Union Report on Licit and Illicit Drugs*, Schaffer Library, 1972. www.druglibrary.org/ schaffer.

Peter Brukner, "Drugs in Sport," *Science Victoria*, October 11, 2001. www.sciencevictoria.org.au.

CBSNews.com, "New Warning on Ephedra," February 4, 2003. www.cbsnews.com.

"Channeling the Energy," Amphetamine Experiences, *Interdope*, n.d. www.interdope.com.

Phillip O. Coffin, et al., "Opiates, Cocaine, and Alcohol Combinations in Accidental Drug Overdose Deaths in New York City, 1990–98," *Drug Text Library Database*, n.d. www. drug text.org.

"Confessions of a White Collar Cocaine Addict: From Ruin to Renewal," n.d. http://home.wi.rr.com.

Mark Court, "Vaccine Hope for Cocaine Addicts," *Times Online*, April 2, 2002. www.timesonline.co.uk.

Cynric, "Jacked: Thirty Hours and Beyond," *Erowid Experience Vaults*, June 23, 2000. www.erowid.org/experiences.

Department of Psychology, University of Buffalo, "Before Prohibition: Images from the Preprohibition Era When Many Psychotropic Substance Were Legally Available in America and Europe," 2001. http://wings.buffalo.edu.

Dinah, "Dinah's Story," *Quit Smoking*, n.d. www.quit-smoking.net/stories.

East Central Minnesota Post Review, "Teen Gives Straight Talk on Addiction," April 2003. www.ecm-inc.com.

Conrad Evarts, "Twelve Hours with a Meth Addict," *Pulp Syndicate,* 2003. www.pulpsyndicate.com.

Parviz Ghadirian, *Sleeping with a Killer: The Effects of Smoking on Human Health,* July 29, 2002. www.hc-sc.gc.ca.

———, "Vintage Wine," n.d. http://cocaine.org.

Good Drug Guide, "Crack Cocaine: A Once-in-a-Lifetime Experience?" n.d. http://cocaine.org.

Greater Dallas Council on Alcohol and Drug Abuse, "Candy Flavored Cigarettes Gain Popularity," April 12, 2002. www.gdcada.org.

Nicole Hansen, "Real Drugs, False Friends: The Nicole Hansen Story," *DrugFreeAZ.com.* n.d. www.drugfreeaz.com.

Antonio R. Harvey, "Stogies Gain Favor with Kids," *Ventura County Star,* June 15, 2001, reprinted on Action on Smoking and Health. www.no-smoking.org.

Pamela Hill, "When High Wears Off, Paranoia, Health Woes Lurk," *Arkansas Democrat-Gazette,* June 7, 1999. www.ardemgaz.com.

Ian Ith, "Cold Pills a Hot Topic in Meth Fight," *Seattle Times,* September 10, 2001. www.mapinc.org.

Jefferson City News Tribune Online Edition, "Illinois' Total Bidi Cigarette Ban Has Teens Primarily in Mind," December 14, 2000. http://newstribune.com.

Kenneth S. Kendler and Carol A. Prescott, "Caffeine Intake, Tolerance, and Withdrawal in Women: A Population-Based Twin Study," *American Journal of Psychiatry,* February 1999. http://ajp.psychiatryonline.org.

Koch Crime Institute, "Methamphetamine Frequently Asked Questions," n.d. www.kci.org.

K.R., "Just Wanted to Have Fun," *CrystalRecovery.com,* n.d. www.crystalrecovery.com.

Jan Landon, "The Meth Trap," *Topeka Capital Journal Online,* November 18, 2001. www.cjonline.com.

Alan I. Leshner, "Oops: How Casual Drug Use Leads to Addiction," *National Institute on Drug Abuse,* January 25, 2001. www.nida.nih.gov.

Lyn, "I Am in Recovery Now, but This Was My Life as an Addict," *Recovery Site*, n.d. http://lynnfromct.freeyellow.com/ addiction.html.

Jonathon Martin, "A Drug's Innocent Victims," *MSNBC News*, 1999. www.msnbc.com.

Medical Online, "Drugs and Drug Abuse: Cocaine," n.d. www.medicalonline.com.au.

Mercola.com, "Ritalin on the Ropes," October 1, 2000. www. mercola.com.

Art Merrill, "Methamphetamine White Lies," *Prescott Valley Tribune*, n.d. www.prescottaz.com.

Mark Moran, "Science Debunks Some Fears About Drug Therapy for Kids with ADHD," *AMNews*, September 6, 1999. www.ama.assn.org.

Mike Mosedale, "Meth Myths, Meth Realities," *City Pages* [Minneapolis, MN], May 14, 2003. www.citypages.com/databank.

Nash, "Excuse Me . . . but May I Have Some More?" *Erowid Experience Vaults*, July 2002. www.erowid.org/experiences.

NBC4.TV News, "Extreme Speed," May 3, 2003. www.nbc4.tv.

Steve Nettleton, "Between a Machete and a Revolver," *CNN.com*, 2001. www.cnn.com.

New Lycaeum, "A Meth Cook Speaks from Prison," September 25, 1995. http://leda.lycaeum.org.

New York State Department of Health, "Thinking About Stopping Smoking?" n.d. www.health.state.ny.us.

NIDA for Teens, "Mind over Matter: Methamphetamine," January 27, 2003. www.drugabuse.gov.

Ken Olsen, "A Health Peril for All of Us," *MSNBC News*, 1999. www.msnbc.com.

Stacey Opland, "Meth Lab Discovered in High School Parking Lot," *Backup Training Corporation*, June 7, 2002. www.the backup.com.

Jim Parker, "Crystal Meth and Other Stimulants: Maximum Speed," *Do It Now Foundation*, October 2001. www.doit now.org.

Carlos A. Perez, "My Kind of Life: Crystal Death—Amphetamine," *Positively Aware*, July/August 2003. www.thebody.com.
Robert Downey Jr., New Beginnings. "An Addict's True Story," n. d. www.geocities.com.
Matthew J. Rosenberg, "Jamaica Struggles to Contain Boom— Coke Smuggling," *Cannabis News*, February 9, 2000. www. cannabisnews.com.
Caitlin Rother, "Doctor Studies Meth's Impacts on Children," *San Diego Union Tribune*, February 10, 2003. www.linde smith.org.
David Satcher, "A Call for Action: Surgeon General's Report, Reducing Tobacco Use," April 3, 2003. www.cdc.gov.
Matt Schofield, "Addict, Area Take Steps to Handle Problem," *Kansas City Star*, November 12, 1998. www.kcstar.com.
Andrew Scutro, "The Meth Behind the Madness," *Idaho Mountain Express*, April 22, 1998. www.mtexpress.com.
SFJ, "My Addiction and Recovery," Addiction and Life Page, Fall 2002. http://pub157.ezboard.com.
Robert Shmerling, "Are There Grounds for Concern?" *Harvard Commentary Health News*, May 25, 2001. www.intelihealth. com.
Sky, "My Story," *Meth Madness*, 2002. www.methmadness.com.
Angela D. Smith, "Alternatives to Jail Time," *SunLink.com*, n.d. www.thesunlink.com.
Cabell Smith, "Medical Uses for Nicotine," *Dukemed News*, August 10, 2001. www.dukemednews.duke.edu.
Julia Sommerfield, "Beating an Addiction to Meth," *MSNBC News*, 2003. www.msnbc.com.
Jessa Sowa, "Green Schools," *Corvallis [OR] Gazette Times*, March 1, 2003. www.gazettetimes.com.
Steven, "The Party's Over," *Tweaker.org*, n.d. www.tweaker. org/stories.
"Success Stories," *Welcome to Mrs. Wilson's*, n.d. www.mrswilsons.org.
Neil Swan, "Brain Scan Opens Window to View Cocaine's Effects on the Brain," *NIDA Notes*, July 1998. www.drugabuse.gov.
Tairona Heritage Studies Centre, "Some Notes on the Use of Coca in South America," 1999. www.lamp.ac.uk.

J.P. Tricot, "Cocaine: Half a Century of Therapeutic Use (1880–1930)," *Verh K Academy, Geneeskd Belgium*, vol. 53, no. 5, 1991. http://cocaine.org.

T.M., "The Shadow People," *CrystalRecovery.com*, n.d. www. crystalrecovery.com.

U.S. Drug Enforcement Administration, "Drug Intelligence Brief: The Forms of Methamphetamine," April 2002. www. usdoj.gov.

Jim Walker, "Hopped-Up Pilots Spark Uproar," *Toronto Star*, August 3, 2002. http://torontostar.com.

Yale University, "Cocaine Use Decreases Ability to Respond to Stimulation, Yale Researchers Find," February 23, 2001. www.yale.edu/opa.

Your Medical Source, "Smoking: How to Stop," n.d. www.your medicalsource.com.

Brad Zellar, "Embedded in Austin," *City Pages* [Minneapolis, MN], May 14, 2003. www.citypages.com.

Websites

BBC News (http://news.bbc.co.uk). This website provides news coverage on a variety of issues related to stimulants.

Do It Now Foundation (www.doitnow.org). Gives general information about illicit drugs and suggests ways for parents to drug-proof their families.

Drug Enforcement Agency (www.dea.gov). Excellent source of information about patterns of drug use in the United States. Also carries news stories relating to drug seizures.

The Good Drug Guide (http://cocaine.org). Offers a variety of articles on the chemistry, methods of use, and dangers of illegal stimulants.

KCI (www.kci.org). Provides information about issues surrounding crime.

National Institute on Drug Abuse (www.nida.nih.gov). Contains research on stimulant abuse and addiction.

Schaffer Library of Drug Policy (www.druglibrary.org/schaffer). Examines the history of drug use and drug policy in the United States.

Substance Abuse and Mental Health Services Administration (www.samhsa.gov). This site provides the results of surveys of past and present drug use.

Tobacco Timeline (www.tobacco.org). Concisely recounts the history of tobacco.

United Nations Office on Drugs and Crime (www.unodc.org). This site provides up-to-date information on the activities on the UNODC.

The Vaults of Erowid (www.erowid.org). A collection of information about illicit drug use, including articles from newspapers, scientific data from research studies, and personal accounts.

WebMD (www.webmd.com). Provides reliable information on a variety of health-related topics.

Index

Picture Credits

About the Authors

Pam Walker received her Bachelor of Science in Biology at Georgia College and advanced degrees in education at Georgia Southern University. Elaine Wood studied biology at West Georgia College and received her graduate degrees in education from University of West Georgia College. They have more than thirty years experience in teaching science in grades seven through twelve.

Ms. Walker and Ms. Wood are coauthors of more than a dozen science-teacher resource activity books, two science textbooks, and a series of middle school books on human body systems.